PENGUIN BOOKS

THE ART OF BEING FABULOUS

Shalini Passi is a Delhi-based art collector, artist and philanthropist. A member of the advisory board of Khoj Studios, a New Delhi-based not-for-profit contemporary arts organization, since 2012 and a long-standing patron of the Kochi–Muziris Biennale, an international contemporary art exhibition held every two years in Kochi, Kerala, she is one of India's most distinctive voices in contemporary art patronage. Her collection spans leading Indian and international artists, including Bharti Kher, Anita Dube, Sheba Chhachhi, Zarina Hashmi, Atul Dodiya, Jeff Koons, Damien Hirst, M.F. Husain, Manjit Bawa and Ram Kumar.

Her passion for art and design extends beyond the canvas—her Delhi home, featured in *Wallpaper, Architectural Digest* and *Larry's List*, is a living gallery that juxtaposes modernist masters with contemporary design by Ron Arad, Vladimir Kagan and Hervé Van der Straeten. Through her foundation, Shalini champions emerging artists and arts education across India. She frequently speaks at leading art and design forums, including the India Art Fair and India Design ID.

She starred in *Fabulous Lives vs Bollywood Wives* (2024), the third season of the popular Netflix reality show *The Fabulous Lives of Bollywood Lives*.

The Art of Being Fabulous

10 RULES *for a* **BEAUTIFUL LIFE**

SHALINI PASSI

PENGUIN BOOKS
An imprint of Penguin Random House

PENGUIN BOOKS

Penguin Books is an imprint of the Penguin Random House group of companieswhose addresses can be found at global.penguinrandomhouse.com

Published by Penguin Random House India Pvt. Ltd
4th Floor, Capital Tower 1, MG Road,
Gurugram 122 002, Haryana, India

Penguin Random House India

First published in Penguin Books by Penguin Random House India 2026

10 9 8 7 6 5 4 3 2 1

The views and opinions expressed in this book are the author's own and the facts are as reported by her which have been verified to the extent possible, and the publishers are not in any way liable for the same.

ISBN 9780143476832

Typeset in Garamond by MAP Systems, Bengaluru, India

www.penguin.co.in

To Dadi Ma and Papaji,

to Sanjay and Robin

and to my eternal muse—Mumbai

Contents

Prologue ix

1. Fabulous Is an Energy 1
2. Inner Strength, Outer Shine 23
3. Fashion as Expression 41
4. Grace, Glitter and Glory 59
5. Immersing in Creativity 85
6. The Art of Giving 111
7. Bonds of a Lifetime 131
8. Living Between Worlds 153
9. Connection with the Divine 169
10. Fabulously Ever After 189

Acknowledgements 207

Prologue

While I was growing up, I felt an inner spark come alive each time I was surrounded by art, creativity, movement and rhythm. In those moments, it was as if I was deeply connected to something larger than myself. I didn't have words to describe it then. All I knew was that it was something real, something that refused to be dimmed.

Much later, I found a word that came close: 'fabulous'.

To me, fabulousness is a form of self-trust, one that begins with how you see yourself, not how the world sees you. It is not the version of you that seeks applause or conforms to trends. Instead, it is the courage to carry your story entirely on your own terms. Above everything else, it is seen in your refusal to shrink, to fit someone else's idea of enough.

Come to think of it, this is the version of fabulousness we have admired in so many public figures. The quiet certainty of Mother Teresa, the courage of Sarojini Naidu, the effortless elegance of Gayatri Devi. You will sometimes also witness it in the most unassuming corners. You may see it in a dancer who lets music move through her uninhibited, in a friend who left everything familiar to build a life she actually wanted and deserved, or in the woman heading back to work after a long break, determined to find her place under the sun.

Fabulousness isn't something you wait to be given. It is something you claim for yourself. It is not a performance, it is a frequency. When you are aligned with it, you don't just walk into a room. You light it up.

✦

People often ask me, 'How do you do it? How do you stay grounded and glamorous? How do you hold your ground and not feel the need to fit in? How do you move through the art world, the fashion world and the public gaze, and still seem so entirely yourself?'

At first, I brushed the question off. I didn't think I had an answer. But over time, I realized that while there is no single answer, there are ways—ways of being that I have grown into. These are ways of seeing, choosing, expressing, caring. Ways I return to when I need to recharge or re-centre.

That is when this book came to life.

Let me be clear from the outset on what this book is, and just as importantly, what it is not.

For starters, this book is not a manual. It is not a list of commandments or rules. It is simply a set of possibilities to explore. If anything, it's a mirror.

Every chapter is a doorway; think of it as an invitation. You will find a chapter each on:

Energy—how you can protect it, and how to trust and amplify it.

Inner wellness—that quiet revolution that keeps you going.

Style—not about following fashion trends, but about developing your own signature.

Fame—on being seen and staying humble.

Creativity—because that is the raw material of all fabulousness.

Philanthropy—not seen as charity, but as an empowered expression of self.

Relationships—both the tender and the transformative.

Bridging worlds—because we are never just one thing.

Spirituality—which, for me, is the backbone of all clarity and joy.

Legacy—not as a monument, but as meaning.

These are the ten ways I have learnt to be fabulous. Not through outside validation, but through a deep, ongoing conversation with myself. Let me give you a head start as you start reading this book.

Some chapters will feel like a memoir, deeply personal, intimate and reflective. Others may feel like a manifesto, a call to reclaim who you are. Some may read like letters scribbled in the margins of life. All of it is true and all of it is me. If you find a piece of yourself here, then it is yours too.

You can read these chapters in any order you like. Read what calls out to you on a certain day. Feel free to take what you need and skip what you don't. In all this, I am not saying, 'Do it like me.' I am saying, 'Find what feels true for you.' If anything, I offer these life events and thoughts with openness, not authority. I would like you to think of it as a shared spark, not a fixed script that you have to follow.

While I am at it, let me add that this book isn't a flawless blueprint either. That is because my own life, like anyone else's, is a patchwork of grace and clutter. There are days I move with clarity and intention. There are other days when I struggle with half-formed thoughts, when I second-guess decisions that might have looked confident from the outside. Like everyone else, I have had occasions when I have said yes when I should have stood my ground, and times when I have said no because fear kept me from saying yes.

But amidst all this, the one thing I have never done is give up on myself. That, to me, is the most fabulous thing of all. After all, fabulousness isn't about getting it right all the time. It is about returning to yourself, again and again. It is the discipline to care for yourself. It is also the courage to change. It is the clarity to say, this is who I am today, and I love her enough to let her evolve.

✦

If you have ever felt 'too much', this book is for you.

If you have ever been told you are too emotional. Too quiet. Too loud. Too confident. Too curious. Too bold for your age. Too soft for your setting. Too feminine for your ambition. Too unconventional to be taken seriously . . . you are the reason I wrote this book.

Because I have been that girl, that woman whose energy doesn't quite fit, doesn't blend or behave. But you know what, I have come to believe that not fitting in is often the first sign that you are onto something real. It has never felt like a burden to me—if anything, it has been an enjoyable ride. The world will always have opinions about how you should be. Fabulousness begins when you stop looking for external approval. When you realize your voice is not meant to echo, it is meant to resonate.

I believe that when even one person comes alive to their energy, it somehow encourages others to do the same. Let us give each other that encouragement. For as much as fabulousness is an individual performance, it is also courage that is contagious.

Chapter 1

Fabulous Is an Energy

The Sound of Silence

My grandmother prayed in silence. There were no accompanying bells or loud chants. There was just a quiet hum that felt like it had wrapped itself around the day comfortingly, like a soft shawl. She could be in the kitchen, cooking one of her delicacies for me, or folding a sari, and just like that, she would slip into prayer—both for herself and for the world.

I think that was the first time I truly witnessed what positive energy could look like. The fact that I grew up in a home where religion wasn't about ritual but about being a good person, made a deep impression on me. My grandparents often repeated the philosophy *tu bhala toh jag bhala*—if you are good, the world is good. That phrase has stayed with me throughout life and has become my quiet inner voice. Watching my grandmother move through her day with quiet intention, I learnt that presence is power. Today, when people ask me what makes someone truly fabulous, I tend to think of stillness. For me, fabulousness is about how you carry yourself, through the highs and the lows, with a certain kind of grace.

While I was growing up in Delhi in the 1980s, my world was a beautiful contradiction. On the one hand, I was surrounded by the deeply traditional values of my grandparents, who upheld the philosophy of 'simple living, high thinking'. On the other hand, I was a child who just couldn't sit still. If there was a song playing, I wanted to dance. If I saw a colour, I wanted to paint with it.

I studied at Modern School, Barakhamba Road, in Delhi, which took great pride in its perfect mix of Indian ethos and modern education. It was here that my first sparks of creativity were lit. We were encouraged to take up every sport, every performance, every possibility. Participation was the culture, not the exception. You got points for being involved, and while many of us began just for the points, we stayed for the passion. There was always something happening, be it sports, theatre, annual day performances or debates. That rhythm of engagement taught me early that creativity isn't a one-time act. It cannot be anything less than a way of life.

Importantly, at school, the arts were valued. I had the opportunity to paint, to sing, to perform, and I responded with equal enthusiasm. My art teacher, Bishamber Khanna, shaped my earliest understanding of aesthetics and detail. He saw something in me and nurtured it with care. Interestingly, he also never gave me top grades. While others received straight As, I would often get a B+. It wasn't because I was underperforming, but because he judged me by my own potential. 'I'm not grading you against them,' he once explained. 'I am grading you against what you are capable of.' That was a life lesson. I learnt early that I didn't have to compete with anyone else.

That same theme showed up in other incidents too. I recall an instance when the school was selecting students for the diving team. The standard process was to start small—one metre, then three, five, seven point five, and eventually progress to ten. Most kids took weeks to build the courage to move up. After I had tried a few jumps from the lower boards, one day my coach called me aside.

'Come, I want to show you the ten-metre board,' he said. I climbed up, assuming I was just there to observe the seniors dive. The next thing I knew, he pushed me off the ten-metre board. I remember panicking in mid-air, kicking and flailing. But something changed for me in that suspended moment. I straightened my body, aligned my arms and dove straight into the water. When I finally surfaced, shocked and breathless, I asked him why he had pushed me. 'Because you are ready,' came his reply. 'I didn't want to waste weeks waiting for you to get here when I knew you could already begin.'

That was a defining moment for me. It taught me something I have carried ever since, which is that you need not wait for the perfect prep. Sometimes you have to leap and figure it out on the way.

Another precious lesson I learnt at school is that no learning is ever wasted. It was a joy that dawned on me slowly, over many years that everything I learnt, every skill I explored, every craft I dabbled in, had a purpose. Even if it didn't reveal itself immediately, it found its way into my life at just the right time. Whether it was art, singing, cooking or simply how to hold space for someone, each bit of learning eventually wove itself into the fabric of who I am.

It helped that I also came from a family that was artistic and visionary in different ways. My father is a painter, and though he didn't pursue painting professionally, his love for art was something I absorbed instinctively. My grandfather was a builder of city spaces. He constructed several iconic buildings in Delhi, including Doordarshan Bhawan, home to India's national broadcaster and Palika Bazaar, a popular underground market of its time. I therefore grew up watching both brushstrokes and blueprints take shape in the same home. I understood that creativity could manifest as much in concrete as on canvas. I often think back to those days with great fondness for the sheer range of things that I learnt. There was the joy of being immersed in a craft, the value of discipline, the happiness of being seen for what I could do.

Growing up, I often pictured myself as an architect. But there was one tiny snag—maths and I didn't quite get along. That is putting it mildly. In fact, I would often fail in the subject. So I pivoted, choosing art instead. Life, of course, had its own plans and pivots for me.

Changed Trajectory

In our conservative set-up, early marriages were the norm. I remember telling my family early on that since I didn't drink, smoke or gamble, I didn't want to be with someone who did either. They looked at me as though I had asked for a unicorn. 'That is going to be very difficult,' was their instinctive response. But I was clear—this was non-negotiable. The universe conspired to make it come true.

I was all of twenty when wedding bells suddenly filled the air. My marriage was arranged, but it came with its own filmy flair. It all began at a friend's sister's wedding. I was singing and dancing—on a Madhuri Dixit number, no less—when my would-be husband's cousin, who happened to be there, saw me. She ran to her family mid-performance and announced that she had found the perfect girl. That evening, his aunt showed up at the function and asked if my parents would be attending.

When I said yes, she insisted on meeting them. That is how it all came together—between dhols and a dance floor declaration.

Sanjay is the eldest son in his family; he was twenty-eight when we got married, while I was just twenty. We came back home as newlyweds and hit the ground running. While the world saw me as a young bride, I was also a student trying to finish college. Sanjay would wake me at 4 a.m. to get me to study, since I had exams to appear for. At the same time, I stepped into my household responsibilities. I began running the house at the age of twenty—coordinating, managing, truly learning by doing. Truth be told, I didn't even know how to cook, or for that matter, how to turn on the gas. There was no script or manual, but I had a strong desire to be perfect. Looking back, I didn't realize how quickly I had to grow up.

Among other things, I suddenly found myself immersed in a social world I didn't yet understand. We entertained often, and I was still figuring out how to carry myself with confidence and ease. I still remember the whispers—those pointed comments about how I didn't know how to dress, how to host, how to truly belong in that elite world.

But instead of letting these voices define me, I decided to learn. I started with experimenting in the kitchen, playing with ingredients and trying different cuisines. Driven by curiosity and instinct, I was exploring almond flour and almond milk long before they became trends. Each time I travelled, I would speak with chefs, collect recipes, and step into kitchens to observe them. Slowly, I became confident preparing Hyderabadi dishes, Thai curries, Chinese stir-fries, a bit of Mexican cooking and also baking. Cooking, in fact, became a way for me to express myself.

Over time, I came to realize that I was quietly rewriting the narrative around me as I observed and evolved. That didn't mean judgements stopped, but they lost their sting. In fact, I began to enjoy the attention. Not out of defiance, but because I had made peace with standing apart. I had decided that no one else would dim my light.

In hindsight, the one thing that has always anchored me is my desire to learn. In those early days, I recall how

I would cut out articles from magazines and file them to be able to devour them later. There were clippings on paintings that I wanted to recreate, art movements that I wanted to understand, architectural styles that fascinated me. I kept a diary with a list of countries that I dreamed of visiting, museums that I wanted to explore and biographies I hoped to read. Every night, I would sit down to read and reflect. Those blue files still sit in my study today, thick with years of learning. That hunger to understand the world beyond the immediate has never left me. Much later in life, for instance, I hired an English teacher just to master pronunciation—how to say each word with clarity, where to place the emphasis, how to speak so that my voice carried the weight of what I knew. It wasn't about sounding polished for the sake of it. I wanted to do justice to the things I had learnt and honour them with the voice they deserved. Visually, I had always been strong; art had been my forte. But when it came to words, I felt a disparity. I wanted my voice to hold the same power.

A year into our marriage, life took another beautiful turn when Sanjay and I were blessed with our son, Robin.

I was all of twenty-one, and in many ways, if I think back to those days, I can say that I grew up with my child—often fumbling, yet slowly finding my rhythm. I remember being just as excited as Robin about going to Disneyland. In many ways, I was rediscovering my own sense of wonder with him.

Come to think of it, since I was married early, it felt like I had gone from childhood to adulthood without ever passing through youth. That sweet, chaotic, expansive phase of being young and carefree was never really mine to live. But somewhere inside me, that unfinished chapter took root as I experienced childhood with my son, and in many ways, it still colours the way I see the world. People often meet me and say, 'You're like a sixteen-year-old!' Or they laugh and insist, 'You can't be more than eighteen!' They say it with disbelief, and I receive it with a smile, because for me, it's not about looking young, it's about feeling young. That girl who never quite had her moment of youth now lives in me fully. She comes alive every time I dance, every time I discover something new, every time I say yes to something unexpected.

This energy, this eternal youthfulness, is perhaps my greatest gift from within. It is my way of being. If there is one thing I can say with confidence, it is that I am not jaded. I'm not tired. I do not walk through life with a 'been there, done that' attitude. I show up with fresh eyes, with curiosity, with enthusiasm. In fact, that is what keeps me going. Much of what I do today, I do for the little girl I once was. I honour her. I let her dance. I dress up for her, I sing for her. I make sure she's never silenced again. Because somewhere along the way, I realized that if you can carry your childlike wonder into adulthood, you will never run out of magic.

Another thing that deepened after marriage was my spiritual path. My husband is very religious and visits many temples regularly. Initially, I wasn't sure. But over time, I saw the power of prayers, the calm of religious spaces, and how they helped me centre myself. I felt an energy in temples, in churches, in mosques. In people and in places. While this energy uplifted me, I must confess that sometimes it also overwhelmed me. Like it did in that house near the ghats of Varanasi, where I had a full-blown panic attack. I was unaware that I had entered a 'death house'. But even then, even in that chaos, I sensed something real and sacred.

That is the thing about fabulousness. It isn't always glamorous. Sometimes, it is spiritual. Sometimes, it's about saying no to the world so you can say yes to yourself. I have done it in many ways, wittingly or unwittingly, unmindful of what the world has to say about me. Take, for instance, the times that I felt drawn to shave my head while visiting the Balaji temple. Not out of grief or loss but out of total surrender. It changed me. The energies I felt were unlike anything else—powerful, untouched. People, however, whispered at me and stared. But I smiled. Fabulousness, I have come to believe, is not just about adding layers, it is also about shedding them. Until what's left is raw, real and unmistakably *you*.

Above everything else, I have learned to trust my energy. I have a knack for sensing people's vibrations immediately. If something feels off, I walk away. But when I find good energy, I stay, I nurture and I grow.

Karma Collector

The standing joke among my friends is that I am what they call a 'karma collector'. They say what keeps me away from negativity is that I am too afraid to earn bad karma. Maybe they are right. I believe that even intention carries karmic weight, and I try to keep mine clean. This is not to say that I am holier-than-thou or immune to human emotions. Of course, I lose my temper, I get jealous, I make mistakes like everyone else. But I try, as much as I can, to stay mindful. To pause and to choose the higher road even when it is difficult. Because somewhere deep within, I believe every action, every thought, every intention carries a ripple.

Over time, I began exploring this idea more deeply. I undertook past-life regression therapy, trying to make sense of certain events or recurring patterns that felt larger than life. As time unfolded, a quiet conviction began to build in me. I saw people around me, those who had done wrong, receive their consequences swiftly. I also saw those who did good, reap unexpected blessings. It was as if the pace of karma had quickened. I grew up hearing,

'*Jo karega, woh bharega* [Actions have consequences] . . . maybe not in this life, but definitely in the next.' I now began to wonder—what if there is no next birth anymore? What if the reckoning is here and now? This idea, that our karmic bank is being balanced in real time, has truly changed the way I live. If this really is the last go-around, then I want to make it count.

My way of dealing with negative emotions, however, is quite practical. There was a time I found myself wrestling with jealousy. I tried to understand what was behind the emotion. So I read about it, questioned it. There was one insight that shifted everything for me—you are not really jealous of a person, you are jealous of what they have. You admire their success, their home, their presence, their talent. Looked at this way, jealousy is actually misplaced admiration. Is it not? That realization changed how I viewed people. If someone danced beautifully, I no longer saw it as a comparison. Instead, I saw it as inspiration. I would go up to them and say, sincerely, 'I admire this about you.' Sometimes people thought I was being fake. 'Oh, look at her being overly nice or dramatic,' they would say. But what they didn't understand was that I was manifesting a certain talent, even before I knew the term. In perspective, I was actually channeling my admiration into aspiration, wasn't I? If I admired someone's singing, I would try to sing better. If I admired someone's way of speaking, I would observe and refine my own.

There is a caveat here though. You have a right to be jealous only if you are willing to put in the effort yourself. If someone has earned that moment, it is not your to resent. It is definitely yours to learn from.

Throughout my life, presence, purpose and passion have been my compass points. For me, presence means showing up fully, not being distracted. When I'm at a party, I'm at the party. When I'm in Purnia in Bihar, meeting children through my UNICEF work, I am there completely. The purpose, or the why behind everything I do, is about elevating beauty in all its forms. Whether it is curating an art collection, supporting young artists, dressing up, or simply setting a table with care, my purpose is to amplify what is often overlooked. And passion is my fuel. It is why I don't sleepwalk through life. It is why

I will be on a 1.30 a.m. flight back home and still be at my desk by 8 a.m.

Today I live in two modes—a turbo mode, when I am on the move, leaping from project to project, and then the quiet, contemplative moments when I pause and ask myself, what am I putting out into the world? Is it coming from a place of truth?

Of Couture and Colours

I am aware that the first thing many people notice about me isn't my energy, or the work I do, or even my beliefs. It is what I'm wearing. The focus is on the couture, on the colours. I understand that. After all, fashion is the most visible part of our identity. But even there, what most don't realize is that my style isn't curated by trends. It is an extension of my energy, just like everything else I do. I wear what makes me feel alive; I dress to express, not impress.

If I have worn a Cleopatra-inspired outfit, it was because I wanted to channel a certain energy. The oversized clips in my hair are a nod to my childhood self. In all of this, I am not trying to be a fashionista. What I am trying to be is free. Every outfit, every accessory, is a conversation between my inner world and the world outside. Yes, it is bold, it is maximalist. But most importantly, it is mine. Besides, it also acts as a protective shield that keeps people and noise out.

That said, gloss and depth can coexist. People tend to put others into boxes. I refuse to be boxed in. They said red lipstick wasn't for serious women. That glam was shallow. That being too 'extra' meant you weren't deep. I smiled and wore the red lipstick anyway. And then built a foundation, mentored artists and brought craft and culture into the spotlight.

People sometimes say, 'But it's easy for you. You have the privilege.' Yes, I do. And I do not take my privilege lightly. I could have been on a permanent vacation, done the bare minimum. But that's not me. I believe, as Krishna told Arjuna, that we must each do our dharma, our duty. I believe I was born into this life for a reason, and I honour that reason through action, through offering up whatever gifts I have. And had I been born as a dog, I would have been a fiercely loyal one, because I believe in giving myself fully to the role I'm given.

You may choose to disagree, but it is my belief that you do not need money, fame or pedigree to be fabulous. What you need is clarity about what brings you alive. If I had to name a few things people need to cultivate their own version of fabulousness, they would be discipline, the hunger to achieve, working on your strengths, and most importantly, working on your weaknesses. We tend to think of weaknesses as limitations. But I have found that when you start working on what you don't know, the growth, the satisfaction, the energy you feel is quite something. After all, you are turning a lack into power.

The biggest gift I have found is that in a world full of noise, I have learnt to tune into something quieter—my own frequency. It took me years to realize that this energy I carry is my truest form of expression.

Sometimes, I think about that young girl, paint on her fingers, head buzzing with ideas, trying to find her place. What would she say to me today? I think she would smile, wide-eyed, slightly in awe, and say, 'You did it your way. You didn't let the noise change you. You stayed true.' And I would smile back and tell her, 'It was never about arriving anyway. It was about flowing.'

Because in the end, the most fabulous thing you can be is yourself—fully, freely and fiercely.

Chapter 2

Inner Strength, Outer Shine

They told me I would never dance again.

I was all of twenty-one, navigating a beautiful but unfamiliar terrain as a newly minted mother. A tiny human completely dependent on me, sleepless nights, and along with it, a constant pain that simply wouldn't go. It turned out I had injured my tailbone. A visit to a well-known orthopaedic brought little comfort. After examining me, he said, quite matter-of-factly, 'You will need an epidural injected into your spine every six months if you want to be functional.' If I thought that was the end of his pronouncement, there was more. 'No yoga, no dance, no heels,' he added as a parting shot.

My husband and my mother were with me at the consultation. When I quietly got up and left the room, they assumed I had gone to the bathroom to cry. But I didn't shed a tear. Instead, I went to my car, sat still for a moment and then drove straight to my dance class.

That day, I realized two things. One, I would never let anyone dictate the limitations of my body. And two, if modern medicine didn't offer me a path to recovery, I would look for it in traditional wisdom.

This was long before Google had become everyone's doctor on click. I turned to what I had—fading notes from my grandmother's shelf, half-forgotten home remedies and slim books on ancient healing systems, especially Ayurveda. That is how my journey with wellness began.

At my lowest, I remember visualising Bhishma Pitamah, the iconic figure from the Mahabharata, known for his resilience and adherence to his principles, lying on a bed of arrows, surviving by sheer willpower. I told myself, if he could survive that, I could survive this. One thing I was sure of—I wasn't going to live half a life, not at twenty-one and not ever.

That was perhaps the first time I truly understood that the body has its own intelligence. If you cannot fix something directly, you can still support it by strengthening what surrounds it. Armed with this knowledge, I began to build up my back, hips and leg muscles, knowing that they could protect my spine without placing pressure on it. In all of this, yoga became my quiet ally, one stretch at a time.

I also began to look closely at my relationship with food. I realized that while modern medicine focuses on cures, we do not cultivate a culture of prevention. I wanted to understand how food could heal, and once I saw its impact, there was no turning back.

Ayurveda taught me that everybody is different. I learnt that true healing is about restoring balance, not just masking symptoms. Going forward, I started paying attention to things like what cooled the body, what built heat, and what my system needed at any given moment. For instance, I cut out watermelon and cucumber—cooling, watery foods that did not suit my condition. Instead, I embraced ingredients that offered warmth and strength.

I also began making my own *leps* (poultices). Slowly, I built a personal ritual, pieced together with ancestral wisdom—home remedies that had been passed down through generations.

And no, I didn't take antibiotics. In fact, I haven't popped a pill in nearly twenty-eight years now. If I have a fever, I reach for methi (fenugreek) water. If my digestion is off, I turn to ajwain (carom seeds). My kitchen is my pharmacy; one that is potent, time-tested and free of side effects.

These days, people often ask me what I use on my skin. My honest answer is clean food. My mornings begin with a shot of ghee, followed by almonds and walnuts. Then come the juices—beetroot with *amla* and ginger, celery, capsicum, sprout juice, all pulped. These aren't indulgences for me. They are potent nutrient bombs. In every sip, they support skin health, gut strength, immunity and mental clarity. Another thing I never skip is goat curd. Rich in probiotics, it is not only great for gut health, but it also helps keep bones and teeth strong.

Up until 6 p.m., I have raw foods. Don't get me wrong—it is not about deprivation. My meals are filling, just thoughtfully chosen. If I need protein, I will have an egg with roti. In the evenings, it might be chicken broth or a little meat, on days when I am not going to the temple. But everything is at room temperature. I have also designed my meals to be simple and portable—no heating, no plating. Most people assume I am constantly socializing. The truth is that I rarely accept dinner invitations. If I must attend an event, I eat beforehand and leave early. I don't like putting my body through the stress of late-night meals. It has taken me years to find my rhythm, and I am not willing to break it lightly.

Overall, I eat for function, energy and balance. Rarely for taste. In fact, I have cut out anything that spikes my system, be it caffeine or sugar. If my body no longer craves certain foods, it is because I have reconditioned my system to enjoy what truly nourishes it. When you stop overwhelming the senses, the body also stops begging for stimulation. My system, I can proudly say, is now built to serve my life, not to sabotage it.

During the shooting of *Fabulous Lives*, with all the flights I was catching at impossible hours and heading straight into shoots, I slipped a little and started having coffee. I almost immediately noticed the toll. My face felt puffy, my system unsettled. As soon as filming wrapped,

I stopped drinking coffee. I went back to herbal infusions, warm water and rest. My body thanked me.

Another thing I do not do is drink alcohol. I simply never liked the idea of borrowing energy that I would have to pay for the next morning. At parties, if the host insists, I sometimes hold a glass of Champagne and then quietly set it aside. I don't want to experience the after-effects—the dullness, the dip in energy, the regret the next morning. None of these is fun. I would rather stay present and bright. It's easy to get seduced by how something makes you feel in the moment—wine at a party, sugar on a bad day. But I always ask myself one question: *How will this make me feel tomorrow morning? Will I feel foggy?* If the answer is yes, I say no. I would rather be high on life. I want to feel sharp at 7 a.m., creative at 3 p.m., graceful at 9 p.m. I have learnt that nothing steals your shine faster than habits that drain you the next day.

If there is another thing I hold sacred, it is sleep. You can push yourself to eat, you can fake a smile, you can even caffeinate your way through a day, but you cannot fake rest. You either sleep or you don't, and your body knows the difference.

There was a time during the pandemic when my sleep was broken. I felt overwhelmed—not just by what was happening in the world, but by how helpless it made me feel. At one point, I even turned to sleeping pills. But I knew that wasn't a long-term solution. Slowly, I brought myself back. Now I protect my nights fiercely. I journal sometimes. I often practise Ho'oponopono, a Hawaiian healing prayer that helps release lingering tension. I have found in it a potent process of resolving conflict and restoring balance through self-reflection, repentance, forgiveness and gratitude. The core of Ho'oponopono lies in taking responsibility for one's actions and their impact: *I'm sorry. Please forgive me. Thank you. I love you.* These four simple phrases have a way of softening even the sharpest edges of my day. They help me close emotional tabs and sleep lighter.

Importantly, what I have learnt is that true rest doesn't come from pills or blackout curtains. It comes from inner peace. It comes from living in a way that doesn't exhaust your nervous system. It also comes from knowing you haven't hurt anyone, including yourself, in the course of your day.

That restful sleep then transitions into a quiet morning. Before the rush of the day begins, before the phone starts buzzing, I lie still and let chants or meditative prayers wash over me. It allows my mind to soften and my body to settle into the rhythm of the day. That stillness is what sets the tone—and from there, everything else flows.

Of course, all of this is not to say that being aligned with my body means everything have always gone as per plan. Many of my rituals have gone hilariously sideways. Like the time I rinsed out an egg hair mask with hot water in winter—it cooked right onto my scalp and hair. Or the day I slathered haldi (turmeric) on my arms, only to realize I had to wear a short-sleeved outfit for an event. My arms were glowing neon yellow. While the Indian guests nodded in understanding, a concerned foreigner leaned in and asked gently if I had jaundice.

But that's what I love about wellness when it's real. It is messy and lived. It's not a performance for social media or a packaged cleanse or a three-day detox. It is a way of life.

Movement as Medicine

'*Aaj kiska gussa nikal raha hai* [Who are you angry with today]?' There are some mornings when my dance instructor will look at me mid-routine and ask this question, wondering if I am angry with someone. Apparently, the intensity of my moves gives me away. Dance is how I metabolize emotions that don't yet have language. I've cried while dancing; I have laughed. I have also let go of people mid-spin. If you've had a massive fallout with someone, sometimes you can just dance it out. By the time you are done, your mind feels steady.

Movement isn't just about fitness for me—it's also expression and release. It is how I recalibrate my energy. Little surprise then that I devote nearly two hours to movement every day. I begin with free-form dancing that is joyful and makes the heart beat faster and the body loosen up. This is followed by Pilates, which builds strength and structure. It may be quieter, slower, but make no mistake, it is no less powerful. Pilates has taught me that strength doesn't have to be aggressive; it can also be quiet and measured. There is something powerful about breathing through discomfort, knowing that your body won't collapse under pressure.

If I were not to move, I feel it not just in my body but also in my thoughts. I become slower, cloudier. Movement helps me metabolize not just calories but feelings too. Most people don't realize that the body stores the stories the mind can't process yet. Movement lets those stories move through. It gives the emotion somewhere to go.

I often say that the world responds to a woman who is fully in her body. You can see it in her posture, in her gaze, in her overall presence. There is a glow that no makeup can replicate.

After I dance, after I move, after I stretch and sweat and breathe, one thought always floats through:

This is what joy feels like in the body.

Come to think of it, this is the same woman who was once told she wouldn't be able to dance or wear high heels.

Emotional Energy Is Sacred

I was in the middle of a therapy session when an earthquake hit Delhi. My therapist, speaking from another city, heard about it and immediately offered to end the call. But I stayed calm. I picked up my phone, called my team and instructed them to move to safety, all the while keeping the session going. Years ago, I might have absorbed the fear and even spiralled with the situation. But now I could hold space for myself and for others without losing my centre.

That kind of steadiness didn't come to me overnight. It came from learning that emotional energy is sacred. It is not something you throw around lightly. You don't need to react to every ping or explain yourself to everyone. That is why I guard my time and my thoughts with a quiet ferocity.

People don't talk enough about *emotional food*—but I believe we consume energy just as we consume meals. Inflammatory news, social media, gossip—all of it affects your system. This is the exact reason why I have not watched the news in over a decade. The way television news is presented today—sensational, relentless—is enough to give you a jolt in the chest, even palpitations, a sudden heaviness. The constant urgency, the catastrophizing, the noise, it cannot make you wiser. If anything, it only makes you wearier. If there's something I truly need to know, I read it selectively on my own terms, on an app. I try to curate what I let in—silence over noise, solitude over sensationalism, and most importantly, alignment over approval.

I must confess, while filming *Fabulous Lives*, there were moments when the world around me felt heightened. That is when I paused, took a deep breath and reminded myself that you are here to show up as yourself. It wasn't that I was resisting the environment; I was trying to stay rooted in who I am.

When I was younger, I used to worry about being left out. About missing a party, about not being seen. But over time, I learnt something life-changing: fabulousness is not about being seen by everyone. It is about being seen by yourself. If you have a strong inner compass, you don't need someone else's map, do you?

When it comes to my relationships, I try to keep things simple there, too. There was a time I would lose sleep over a comment someone made. I would dissect every word someone said or didn't say. One night—and I remember this clearly—I was pacing around at 3 a.m., worked up over something someone had said. That's when something in me snapped. I thought to myself: *This isn't peace. And peace is what I choose now.* So I made a simple rule. If I can fix it, I'll fix it. If not, I will let it go. I won't let it fester. In times when letting go feels hard, I fall back on something that's never failed me—karma. I genuinely believe that people who act out are often hurting and that life has its own way of restoring balance. I just do my part, then step out of the way.

As a creative person, I've learnt the hard way that emotional chaos seeps into your spirit. It dulls your light, and I refuse to let that happen to me. Creativity is like the wings of a butterfly—beautiful, fragile and easily bruised. Touch it too much, and you damage the very thing you admired.

Above all, I remind myself that you cannot create beauty if you are exhausted inside. You certainly can't be fabulous if you're falling apart emotionally. Can you?

Energy, Alignment and Everyday Magic

By 2018, I had hit some kind of a wall. My son was off to university, and while I had devoted long years to raising him and to my own wellness and inner balance, something in me had begun to stir. I felt ready for a new purpose—something more meaningful, something that aligned with service. That's when I reached out to my Guru for guidance. His words were simple but life-altering: 'Do higher work.'

Those three words shifted something in me. I realized that everything I'd built—my sensibility, my experiences, my resources were meant to be used in service. But I needed the energy to match the vision. So, I began to pray—not for fame or recognition, but for physical and mental strength. I said: *God, give me the energy of a thirty-five-year-old.* Slowly, but surely, I began to see changes.

My muscles tightened, my posture changed. There was a new lightness in my movement. There was also a new groundedness in my mind.

When I could feel that divine generosity at work, I further dared to ask: *Could I also have the energy of a twenty-five-year-old?*

When you say to the universe: *Give me strength and I'll put it to good use*, something opens up. You experience magic.

Wellness isn't something that I 'returned' to. It's something I have built upon—layer by layer, year by year. To this end, 2018 wasn't a course correction. It was simply an expansion. It was a shift from personal healing to public purpose. It was the moment my inner discipline became outward-facing; the moment my body became a channel.

I can say with pride today that I didn't arrive at this place by accident. I made conscious choices; I worked towards protecting my energy. That is the thing about fabulousness. You work for it, and then it becomes the fuel that powers your presence.

If you ask me today, where does my glow come from? It is from that prayer I sent up to the divine in 2018. It comes from that moment when I first said, *Give me strength, and I will serve.*

To anyone who is looking for a magic bullet for fabulousness, I will confidently say that your habits are that magic bullet. The glow comes from your daily rituals; your inner alignment is the real flex.

Chapter 3

Fashion as Expression

Maximalist, Maverick, Me

Minimalism may be having its moment in design circles, but it has never been the way India lives. We are a culture of abundance—layered, expressive, unapologetically maximalist in the most glorious way.

From Kashmir to Kanyakumari, we are wrapped in tradition, drenched in colour, adorned with meaning. Our expression lives in the details. It is seen in what we wear, how we celebrate, the rituals we hold dear. Nothing about the way we live is half-hearted. Our festivals erupt in colour. Our weddings unfold over days. Our cooking is a symphony of flavours. We dye our fabrics in turmeric, indigo and blood orange. Even our greetings are generous gestures that are warm and expressive.

I tend to carry this same maximalist energy into my style. I dress like I live—with layers, with stories stitched into every fold. I take pride in the fact that my style is deeply intuitive and unapologetically mine. It makes a statement on its own terms, without needing validation from trends or other people. But here's the thing—I have never thought of myself as a fashionista. In fact, I don't even read fashion magazines, let alone chase trends.

That said, I do go through phases when I am drawn instinctively to certain textures or colours. I may gravitate towards prints, not because they are trendy, but because they carry emotion. A particular flower might remind me of someone I love, or of a place I once wandered. A Japanese wave print can transport me back to a museum in Kyoto. A bold chintz might evoke stories of colonial trade, of craft, of quiet resilience.

But it wasn't always this way.

There was a time—largely between 2009 and 2018—when my wardrobe was completely black and white. Monochrome. Minimal. Stripped to the bare essentials. It mirrored my inner landscape—serious, contemplative, rooted in a deep sense of responsibility and quiet intensity. I think shaving my head at Tirupati Balaji had something to do with it. It was an act of surrender, of letting go, of clearing space both within and without. With a buzzcut, there was no room for ornamentation anyway. My clothes were pared back. My earrings were tiny studs. There was no colour or drama, just stillness.

That season of stillness taught me something invaluable. That is why, when I returned to colour, it wasn't for spectacle, it was for its meaning. Dressing, for me, has always been about showing up in something that holds a story. I feel textiles are an important part of how India speaks, be it a Banarasi brocade or raw silk from Assam. I often find myself building entire looks around a single weave or embroidery. It is my way of honouring the craft, of letting the garment speak. Very often, I am not just wearing fashion—I am wearing Indian art. People often ask me, 'Do you ever repeat clothes?' The answer is, all the time. I have saris that are over thirty years old, suits embroidered in the style of another era.

Just as style can preserve the past, it can also rise up to the demands of the present. That is what I felt when I dressed for the MASH Ball—the moment many remember from *Fabulous Lives*. The MASH Ball is a charity gala I conceptualized to bring people together in support of children—the most vulnerable members of our global community. The funds we raised went to UNICEF's Art-Based Therapy and Early Childhood Development programmes, initiatives I believe in deeply. I have always wanted to do my bit to empower individuals to use their influence, resources and passion to create positive change in the lives of children. I want to foster a world where every child's rights are upheld, and their future safeguarded. Given the cause, it felt important to show up that day with intention—not just in spirit, but in presence too.

I remember some friends joking before the ball, 'You are sure to arrive in a white gown, dressed like an angel.' To be honest, that was actually my initial plan. It also made me wonder if I had become predictable. The more I thought of it, though, something made me pause. That night, I realized what I actually wanted was to embody the strength and beauty of empowered womanhood. It is with this thought that I started looking at portraits of women through history—women who weren't just admired but revered; women who carried a certain charisma. That is when Cleopatra captured my imagination. There is only one word I have for her—'regal'. Inspired by her, I stepped into gold regalia, complete with headgear. I wore it not as a costume, but as a mood, a declaration. It was my way of honouring parts of myself that don't whisper. That is the beauty of style; it lets you choose both the volume and the message you want to convey.

While for the MASH Ball my message was bold, at other times it can be equally playful. Like the time I carried a phone-shaped bag to a TV show—a big, bold telephone. I had been told no phones were allowed on set, so I brought one as a fashion accessory. It wasn't just a statement; it was a wink. Just like the sparkly hair clips I have worn. They remind me what it feels like to shine in small, defiant ways.

I believe fashion gives us permission to do both—to honour where we come from, and to play with who we are becoming. So yes, you can smile at the phone bag or raise an eyebrow at the gold cuffs. As long as you don't miss the message: You need to dress for yourself. If your outfit reflects your mood, your energy, the whole room picks up on that. It is not about seeking approval; it is about finding alignment. Many people tell me how they avoid dressing up on days when they feel low. But I always say that is when it matters most. Bring out that gold cuff, the red lipstick. Not to impress the world, but to remind yourself of your own power.

While on the subject of dressing up, I have to confess something—I love ugly shoes. In fact, the chunkier, the better. I can't bear to be slowed down by delicate heels or fussy sandals. I walk fast—really fast—and I need my shoes to keep up. My wardrobe works backwards; I often start with the shoes and then build the outfit from there. Long, sweeping dresses may hide the shoes beneath. While others see elegance, for me, there is freedom to move, to explore.

'You always wear the same shoes,' a friend once teased me. The fact is, I do not need variety for variety's sake. If anything, I need consistency with character. Comfort, to me, is not negotiable. And style certainly should not come at the cost of mobility. I remember even at Cannes, while others glided around in five-inch stilettos, I zipped my way through. That pace is an intrinsic part of who I am.

Wearing India at Cannes

Speaking of Cannes, it was an experience I truly hold close to my heart. It brought together everything I care about: art, culture, storytelling and presence.

When people first called it my 'red-carpet debut', I remember smiling to myself. I didn't even know there was such a thing. I have lived many creative lives, that of an artist, collector, patron, dreamer. So for me, this didn't feel like a beginning or an arrival. In fact, it felt like a continuation, another page in an otherwise full story. This is not to say I didn't understand the fascination—the world sees red carpets as high-glamour stages. And Cannes, of course, has its rich history.

My first impression there, however, was nothing like the movies. It was noisy, unpredictable, frenzied. Stars were arriving, paparazzi were shrieking, fans were jostling for selfies and autographs. I even briefly remember thinking: *Why am I here?* But by the end of it, I was hooked. Cannes has that kind of electricity. More than anything else, it made me deeply grateful that I could show up on my own terms.

For me, Cannes was far more than fashion. It was a celebration of art in all its forms. And most importantly, I felt privileged to be carrying India with me. I didn't see my outfits as just couture; they were cultural storytelling. I wanted the world to see that India isn't just a place; it is something larger than life, an experience.

As someone deeply committed to elevating Indian art on the global stage, I was honoured to be part of collaborations that brought together the best of our creative traditions. One of the experiences I hold dear was wearing a custom gown created by the celebrated fashion designer Manish Malhotra that featured breathtaking artwork by the Padma Shri awardee artist, Paresh Maity. Wearing it, I felt as though I was carrying a fragment of India's geography, history and soul. Inspired by the landscape of the country—from Kashmir to Kanyakumari—that gown wove together textile, craft and artistic spirit in the most immersive way.

I will admit that I had a few doubts at the beginning about how that gown would shape up. Paresh's original painting is monumental. My fear was that what comes alive on a flat canvas may not translate easily into couture. I asked myself, would the scale overwhelm the garment? Would the details get lost in the folds? Would the essence survive?

One thing I knew, though, was that I was in the best hands. And when that gown came together, it put all my doubts to rest. It was breathtaking, to say the least. To put it simply, it was a moving canvas, a convergence of art, fashion and heritage. That gown held the entire cultural map of India, and my own emotional journey, in its folds.

Just as everything was falling beautifully into place, I experienced what was perhaps a signature dose of red-carpet drama. A last-minute rule declared that long trails were no longer allowed on gowns. I wasn't too worried about the announcement. After all, mine wasn't too extravagant, and besides, I was sure I had seen far longer ones sweep by. Only when I reached the security checkpoint did the shock come. I was stopped by a guard. 'Your trail is too long,' he said. 'You cannot go.'

I was stunned. But instead of panicking, I decided to act. I turned to my team and made a simple gesture: 'Get me scissors.' Perhaps knowing me, they even had some on hand. And just like that, in front of the crowd, we removed the train as a couple nearby held the fabric. 'You have nerves of steel,' I heard someone whisper. But to me it wasn't a dramatic act. It was the most practical thing to do—a quiet decision to move forward. The irony, however, wasn't lost on me. In complying with the rule, we had cut through the Indian Ocean, a symbol of vastness and continuity. The show, however, had to go on.

That moment taught me an important lesson: style isn't always about control. Sometimes it is also about surrender. Importantly, the message was that nothing could take away from what mattered most—the pride of showing that Indian couture can hold its own on a global red carpet. It wasn't just fashion. It was storytelling, through fabric and form. That day, I wasn't just representing myself. I was carrying a country's soul—expansive, expressive, rich in texture and tradition.

Six Yards of Strength and Storytelling

If there is one other garment I loved wearing at Cannes, it has to be the saree. Why just at Cannes? I have worn it everywhere. That sense of carrying India, of wearing my heritage as a presence, has found its truest expression in the saree. To me, the saree signifies both femininity and strength. It is not just a garment—I think of it as grace and grit in a single drape.

I remember wearing my first saree at fifteen, a graceful, flaming orange for a cousin's wedding. I remember feeling grown-up, even a little powerful. Later, I wore sarees to school functions, to college events. Somewhere along the way, it became a marker of becoming. It saw me through from girlhood to womanhood. Friends would often ask me, 'Why do you wear sarees so often?' Well, because I felt most myself in them. How could it be any other way for me? After all, I had grown up watching my mother, grandmothers and aunts wear sarees with elegance and ease. I used to peek into my grandmother's cupboard just to marvel at her Banarasis and hand-painted silks. Those sarees weren't mere clothes —they were living heirlooms. Those sarees could tell timeless stories from weddings, travels and other rituals.

Living in Delhi, when I have to move from a wedding to a formal dinner to a political event in one evening, the saree always fits the bill. It offers both dignity and comfort. Even at Cannes, when I sat on formal panels, I often chose the saree. It was not to make a statement, but because it felt most natural to me. In fact, I recall another moment at Cannes that beautifully captured its effortless grace. I was headed to the India Pavilion for a talk with Paresh Maity, wearing a saree, of course. As luck would have it, traffic came to a complete standstill. Cars were not moving, but time was slipping by. I looked around and instinctively said, 'I'm not sitting through this. I'm walking.' People were stunned. 'But you are wearing a saree!' they pointed out. To which I smiled and said, 'Exactly. Watch me,' as I began to walk.

Unknown to me at the time, more drama awaited. It soon started raining—fast and heavy. I ducked under a shopfront, waiting it out. Somewhere along the way, we even did an impromptu shoot—because why not make some memories out of mayhem? Ten minutes later, the skies cleared. By then, my car had caught up, and I stepped back in, reaching the pavilion in time. That moment summed up everything I love about the saree—its power and its playfulness. It is as perfect for a red carpet as it is for a seaside stroll, ice cream in hand.

Draping a saree, I believe, is also an art form. Just as origami is revered in Japan, the saree is India's own wearable sculpture. It is not just about the fabric—it is about movement, about meaning. I am delighted that global designers are beginning to see the beauty of the drape. You see hints of it in capes, in sashes. I appreciate it all, but for me, the classic six-yard saree is perfection in itself. I really think it doesn't need reinvention. But that is just me. To Gen Z, I say, don't let anyone tell you the saree is too traditional, too complex, too slow. It is a blank canvas. Wear it with sneakers, with crop tops, jackets, belts. Just drape it your way. You don't need a stylist—all you need is imagination. Because in the end, perfection isn't the goal—expression is. In fact, fashion doesn't need you to follow any rules. If anything, fashion needs to follow you.

If there is anything that quietly kills that spark, on the other hand, it is conformity. I remember before

Fabulous Lives aired, everyone had a piece of advice for me. 'Highlight your hair, it's too dark. Lighter shades are trending,' they said. I will admit, I even considered their suggestion.

I called a colourist. 'How much time will it take to colour my hair?' I asked.

'Two, maybe two and a half hours,' he said. 'And then you will need touch-ups every forty days.'

I had my answer right there. 'No, thank you,' I said instinctively. I don't have that kind of time or inclination. If I am going to spend hours on something, let it be curating an exhibition, mentoring a young artist, or building something that leaves a mark. So instead, I decided, as always, to twist my hair back, pin it up and move on with my day. I have kept my natural texture and colour—something real, something I have inherited. Besides, I would rather have a full head of unprocessed hair at the end of my life than brittle breakage from blow-dries and bleach.

That apart, these days when I scroll through Instagram, it feels like déjà vu. You see the same waves, the same balayage, even the same faces. That sameness, to me, doesn't feel fabulous. Instead it feels fatiguing. Looking good shouldn't mean looking like everyone else, should it?

Take Up Space

Turns out, being unapologetically yourself can also be the boldest trend of all. I couldn't ever have imagined that one day, young girls would be throwing *Sassy Passi*-themed parties—complete with bold makeup, maximalist prints, glittering accessories and dramatic entrances. But apparently, it's a thing. I have seen the reels; even had the invitations. It is all a bit surreal, and honestly, also a bit funny.

What I am very clear about is that when young women channel their inner 'Passi,' they're not trying to be me. What they are actually reaching for is a version of themselves that feels bolder, freer, more alive. They are trying to be fearless, unapologetically their own. I have to admit that I love that.

If my sense of style gives someone else permission to go bigger, bolder, more individualist . . . fabulous.

I would say wear the clip, paint the eyeliner, carry that bag. Importantly, take up space. That's the whole point. Isn't it?

Chapter 4

Grace, Glitter and Glory

For the longest time in my life, I avoided the camera as if it were out to get me. It wasn't really shyness. I just didn't see myself as someone made for the lens. I didn't know my angles, didn't obsess over my 'best side,' and frankly, I didn't care to. My world was more tactile—art, design, ideas—not selfies and screen time.

I remember a chance encounter with the legendary film-maker Yash Chopra ji at a friend's dinner. I must have been all of twenty-one at the time. I entered the venue wearing my favourite attire, a saree. He looked at me warmly and said, 'You are the quintessential Yash Raj film heroine, you should act.' It was such a generous compliment. I remember being really touched and thanking him with all my heart. But I also told him honestly, 'I am far too camera-conscious.' And I truly was. The very idea of performing for a lens made me uneasy. It just never felt like my space.

Up until 2018, if you had shoved a camera in my face, I would have looked like a deer caught in headlights—stiff, silently praying it would all just go away. I even went to absurd lengths to avoid the camera. If a magazine happened to take my photo, I would sometimes call and request that they not use it. That is how uncomfortable I was with being seen.

Part of it, I think, was aesthetic discomfort. I didn't like how the camera caught me. I felt it was too intense, too sharp. I always felt there was no softness in the gaze, no nuance. It felt jarring, as if I were being misrepresented by the image.

That unease, I realize now, went back further than I thought. Even in school, I had no real interest in either being in front of or even behind the camera. I gravitated towards everything else—painting, craft, sculpture, clay modelling, dance, art, debate. But photography never called to me. I still remember walking past the darkroom and being immediately put off by the smell of developing rolls. There was a sharp, chemical odour that lingered, and with it, my disinterest. While most of my peers associated the camera with magic or memory, it just wasn't my thing.

Looking back, there was an even deeper reason why I didn't want to face the camera. In hindsight, I see it may have been a quiet rebellion. For years, I dressed conservatively, keeping myself fully covered because I didn't like people commenting on my 'porcelain skin' or viewing me only through the lens of appearance. I wanted to be taken seriously for my convictions, for my creative work, for the causes I championed, not for these surface-level impressions. Maybe that is why stepping into the camera's gaze felt so radical.

But somewhere along the way, the world had begun to change. Interviews were shifting from print to video. Visual media was becoming the dominant language. And at the same time, something inside me was shifting too.

In February 2018, I shaved my head during a visit to Tirupati Balaji. It was an act of spiritual reset, though not the first time I had done it. In the past, however, whenever I shaved my head, I would make it a point to retreat from the world for two or three months. I would slow everything down and immerse myself in silence and introspection. This time was different. The India Art Fair was the very next day. International guests were arriving. There was no way I could skip the opening dinner.

My options were limited. I didn't want to wear a headscarf—that would, in all probability, lead most people to assume that I was unwell. So I did what any slightly dramatic but enterprising woman might do—I ordered a wig. This one was from France. *Très chic*, you might say . . . only, they sent me a blonde wig. I had no option but to walk into the art fair wearing it, hoping I didn't attract more attention than the installations. People did double-takes. 'Blonde? Really?' they muttered in surprise. I simply let them wonder.

In my mind, what mattered was that I had shown up. We took hundreds of photos that night, and when I saw them later, I surprised myself. My face looked alive in them. I had stepped into the moment—wig, spotlight and all—and come to think of it, nothing had crumbled.

I think that night I crossed a significant threshold. For once, I hadn't flinched at my own image. For the first time, I wasn't shrinking from the spotlight, I was stepping into it. I also came to a quiet realization: this body, this presence, was given to me by God. I asked myself—why had I been hiding it? If a little glamour could help amplify the work I cared about—whether in art, philanthropy, or in reaching a wider audience, there was nothing wrong. I was now certain that I didn't need to disown beauty in order to be taken seriously. I could claim both, the substance and the shimmer.

Not long after, I launched the digital platform MASH to support artists and showcase interdisciplinary creativity. I knew we had to reach a wider audience, especially the youth. To speak to them—not just about art, but about ideas, aesthetics and possibility—I had to stop hiding behind the scenes. I started taking small steps. The lens that once felt so threatening now became an ally.

Of course, at that time, I didn't know what this shift would open up. I did not know that saying yes to the camera would also mean saying yes to a different version of myself. But that's the thing about change—it rarely arrives with fanfare. It often comes quietly as a soft voice that says: *try*.

And try, I certainly did. I even bought a few books—old-school Hollywood ones on how to pose like a 1950s actress. I watched videos on how to 'romance the camera'. I took notes and practised gestures. What I did, in effect, was stare into the lens until it stopped staring back. I even hired a teacher to fix what I thought was unclear diction—swallowing words, stammering, mispronunciations. Bit by bit, I trained myself to speak with clarity and confidence, not just for the camera but for myself. Somewhere between that first awkward video and the speeches that followed, I found something I hadn't known I was missing—ease.

All of this gave me the confidence to finally pursue a dream I had long held but never felt strong enough to chase: creating my own art and travel show. As an artist, I had always been captivated by the richness of Indian art. For the first time, I felt ready to explore the country's art and architecture through the eyes of a curious wanderer. I shot in several locations and learnt a lot about our country. Along the way, I also had some quirky experiences that are worth telling, if only for the laughter they are bound to evoke.

While in Ladakh, I remember how a strong wind once ripped my outfit mid-shoot. Or that absolutely bizarre moment when a wild yak made its way towards us, seemingly from nowhere, in a split second. One moment, I was engrossed in the shoot, and the next, I was being hit by this yak from behind, while it went running straight into the water. Even though I fell from the impact, I managed to steady myself enough the next moment to ask, 'Did anyone get that on video?' I was keen not to waste the opportunity. Needless to say, my team shook their heads, equal parts concerned and bewildered at my question. 'We were running to save you,' one of them offered, by way of explanation. Moments like this remind you of the unpredictability of real life, making its cameo while you are busy doing other things.

I also filmed in Jaisalmer, where a dust storm lifted my eyelashes right off. It was chaotic, yet exhilarating. Above everything, these experiences helped me build confidence in myself. I learnt that if you lean into the unpredictable and trust it, something beautiful will emerge.

While on the subject of shooting and learning, there is another moment that lingers in my memory. Many years ago, I was persuaded by the legendary designer Rohit Bal to attend a shoot. On the set that day, I happened to meet the legendary actress Shabana Azmi. She was so poised and self-assured—every bit the legend she is. At one point, as the camera turned toward me, I smiled instinctively. Shabana ji looked at me and said, 'Smile like you know everything.' That one line has stayed with me. I think from that time onwards, I began noticing how every smile holds a different energy. That experience also taught me a very valuable lesson—that you don't just pose for the camera, you need to show up with intention and with presence.

Fabulous Lives

I was first approached for a cameo in the finale of *Fabulous Lives* Season 2. I was in London at the time, receiving an award and had to let the opportunity pass. Strangely enough, I had been reading Nissim Ezekiel that week—the Bombay-born poet who studied in London and later returned to teach in Mumbai. Looking back, it feels as though the two cities were having a quiet conversation. Sometimes, life offers you these subtle hints, alignments if you like—only you don't always recognize them until later.

A few months later, the team at Dharmatic Entertainment reached out to me again—this time for Season 3 of *Fabulous Lives.* I remember I was at a party hosted by Manish Malhotra when the conversation with Karan Johar resurfaced. Something about that conversation this time felt different.

By this time, of course, my relationship with the camera had changed. The Shalini who hated being photographed, who would visit the world's most beautiful places and return with albums full of architecture but not a single shot of herself, had started to loosen her grip. I had begun to meet the camera on my own terms, cautiously at first, and then with a kind of practised boldness.

In fact, at the time I had imagined many more outdoor sequences—at the Red Fort, through the grandeur of Lutyens' Delhi, across the many monuments that hold our stories. I felt confident that if we shot there, I could bring something unique to the screen: context, history, a sense of rootedness. The city of Delhi wasn't just a setting for me, it is part of who I am.

While I didn't say yes immediately to the offer, it set me thinking. I thought about the platform, the visibility, the fact that most of the audience were women like me—mothers, wives, dreamers. There would be women, who had perhaps paused pieces of themselves for the sake of family or social expectation, and who needed to see someone like them living a bit freer.

Besides, if I did go ahead, I wouldn't be doing it just for entertainment. I saw the series as a way to expand the space for the work I truly cared about. While developing my travel show, I had been told it could gain traction if I had a stronger public presence. That advice stayed with me. If I wanted to grow that audience, I knew I needed a larger entry point.

Of course, not everyone shared my view. My son, for instance, was convinced I wasn't cut out for reality TV. 'You don't watch TV,' he said. 'You don't gossip. You live in your own world. This isn't for you.' I couldn't say he was wrong. My friends were sceptical too. 'This doesn't feel like you,' they said gently. 'We know that what some might call arrogance is really just your way of protecting your inner world. But not everyone will see it that way.'

While I understood everyone's apprehensions, somewhere deep down, I had already said yes to myself. I wasn't stepping into this to prove anything. I simply wanted to show up fully and on my own terms. For me, it was about being open to the experience, to have fun, to experiment, to see what might unfold.

At the time, though, I was still letting the decision settle quietly, allowing it to take root within before speaking it aloud at home. In fact, it was Gauri Khan, a family friend, who ended up mentioning it to my husband. He didn't miss a beat. 'Of course she's doing it,' he said to her, as if he had known my decision all along.

Walking the Fine Line—Real vs Performed

When I stepped into the Dharma Productions office for the first time, it felt like walking into a new school on my very first day. I felt a strange mix of nervous energy, quiet awe, and of course, wide-eyed anticipation. We have all grown up watching Dharma's films. Many of their stories have shaped our dreams. To be invited into that world, not as a visitor but as someone meant to be there, felt surreal. And yet, it also felt oddly grounding.

The office radiated creative energy. I saw writers huddled over scripts; there were directors exchanging notes. Iconic movie posters lined the walls. The energy in the air was alive and electric. The setting transformed me into a little girl who was starting something new, not knowing where it would lead, but believing that anything was possible.

When the reality of being filmed finally began to sink in, I was inundated with more advice. My son, ever the realist, suggested that I watch a few international reality shows. 'Just so you know what you're getting into,' he said pragmatically. I suspect a part of him was still hoping that viewing these shows might scare me off. Friends weighed in too: 'Record short clips and send them to us. We'll guide you; we'll tell you what works, what to say, how to carry yourself.'

I nodded politely. In fact, I even dutifully queued up the shows my son had recommended. The truth is, I couldn't sit through them for more than a minute or two. I would pause almost immediately. When he walked into the room, I would pretend I was mid-episode, deep in 'research'.

The fact was, I already knew that if I was going to do this, I wasn't going to rehearse it. I wasn't going to perform or play a part that someone else could have scripted better. I wanted to show up as myself—spontaneous, awkward if needed, unfiltered if it came to that.

So there was no prep, no media coach, no 'lines' to hit. I didn't want to carry anyone else's energy into the room. I wanted to walk in with my own energy. I simply wanted to be myself. If I laughed, it would be because something genuinely made me laugh. If I cried, it would be because something moved me. If I stayed silent, it would be because I truly had nothing to say in that moment.

People around me were nervous. 'Your scenes will be edited,' they warned. Others said, 'They'll shape you into a character.' But I wasn't unduly perturbed. I knew the only thing I could control was what I brought to each moment—my energy and my presence. That is all we ever have, and that is what I chose to ground myself in.

If there was one thing I decided early on, it was that I wasn't going to make fun of anyone else on air. If humour was needed, and it often is in such formats, it would be at my own expense. I have always believed that if you make fun of yourself, no one gets hurt. That was my approach: to show up, bring a little lightness, entertain if I could, but never at someone else's cost.

There's a line I have always loved from Raj Kapoor's *Mera Naam Joker*: *'Kehta hai joker saara zamaana . . . aadhi haqiqat, aadha fasana.'* Half truth, half fantasy—but the joke's always on the joker. Somehow, that felt just right.

What helped, in the intervening days, to keep any second thoughts at bay was that I was deeply immersed in my own work. I was planning the MASH Ball, travelling, working on art collaborations and more. My life didn't pause for the show; I just folded the shoot into it. That, I think, kept me anchored.

Choosing Lightness Over Cynicism

When the shoot began, what struck me almost immediately was that the camera never lies. It catches everything—from the flicker of doubt to the unspoken reactions. There is, in fact, a strange intimacy to being followed by the camera. It may feel invasive, but it is also deeply reflective.

That said, of course, there were moments of hesitation. I would sometimes catch myself wondering should I have worn something trendier? Should I have delivered a punchier line, added more flair? But every time I felt that tug to play to the gallery, I stopped myself. *You're not here to impress,* I'd remind myself. *You are here to express.* That one reminder changed everything.

I also kept in mind the women who might be watching the show. I told myself that authenticity can be its own kind of power. That you can be soft and still be formidable. That, to me, is real fabulosity.

People assume that to be camera-ready means spending hours in hair and makeup, scheduling Botox appointments, having stylists put together a high-gloss version of yourself.

I refused that path, simply because I didn't want the version of me on screen to feel like a wax figure. I wanted to show up as I am, expressive and alive.

Importantly, I relied on my own version of glamour—Delhi-style *jugaad*. We are a city that loves to fix things on the fly. So when my hair went frizzy, I didn't panic or call in for a blow-dry. Instead, I clipped my hair up. That is how my now-recognisable look was born. It came not from a stylist's kit, but from a moment of practical improvisation. To me, glamour has never been about polish alone, it is more about presence.

Another thing I came to realize is that the presence of a camera shifts the energy in any room. It doesn't necessarily create anything false, but it can amplify, it can turn the volume up on emotions, expressions, reactions. When the atmosphere tipped into high drama, I tried to choose stillness over spectacle. On one such evening, I quietly said, 'I'd rather walk into the ocean.' That is what I did, I returned to calm when everything around felt charged. To be honest, I wasn't interested in winning the moment. What I was interested in was keeping my peace. That quiet walk into the water became my answer. It was a gesture of defiance and surrender all at once. When emotions run wild, the ocean holds space. It doesn't shout, it soothes.

While I speak of the ocean, it will also be interesting to recount what my favorite moment during the shoot of the series was. In fact, it is a question that I have often been asked. I think it will have to be an off-camera moment, which was perhaps more cinematic than anything that aired. We were told early on that during filming of the series, we would be heading to an ocean destination. We didn't know it would be Mauritius until much later. But the moment I heard 'ocean', I began preparing, knowing that I would want to take the opportunity to scuba dive. I had first learnt to dive with my husband and son and loved the experience. Determined to do it right this time, I even began training in a Delhi pool—in the middle of winter—just to reacquaint myself with the rhythm of the water.

When we reached the island, the weather, however, was playing truant. It was stormy, rain lashed the shores. Everyone was sceptical and wondered, 'Should we go ahead?' I, however, knew that I had to do this. That particular dive was tough. The waves were wild, the current was choppy. I even threw up before I jumped in. As I entered the water, I could not see anything below. To add to it, the oxygen tank slammed into my ribs. But I was determined to keep going. There is something incredibly humbling about being that close to nature. The drama we have on land, those complicated conversations, the tensions and misunderstandings, all of them seem to dissolve in the vastness of the water. The ocean makes everything else feel . . . well, small. It does not just wash over your body; it also scrubs your energy clean. I find it extremely healing.

That dive reaffirmed my belief that I was not there to perform. I was there to anchor into my own stillness, my own clarity.

Seen, Heard, Felt

While shooting for the series had its moments, nothing—absolutely nothing—could have prepared me for the response that came after it aired. When the season dropped, everything seemed to change overnight. I had thought that once the series aired, I would return to my old life, to my work, my art. I expected a few polite messages, maybe some light banter in social circles. What I didn't expect was an avalanche.

For the first six to eight months, I received hundreds of DMs every single day. They came not just from India but from across the world—Canada, South Africa, the Middle East. Teenagers, parents, middle-aged professionals and members of the queer community all wrote in. They also received tons of messages from women who had been bullied, from men who felt invisible. Messages were flowing in from people who felt like misfits, and who were now rejoicing, finally seeing someone on screen who was not trying to fit in.

A young woman wrote to me: 'I always thought something was wrong with me. But after watching you, I realized it wasn't me. It was their insecurity.' Different variations of that message poured in, each one echoing the same quiet relief. Another woman wrote: 'I watched the series for the drama, but I stayed for your energy.' The most touching notes came from women who saw parts of themselves in me—the ones who said, 'You have made being soft and strong look possible.'

There were also encounters in person, and these often caught me completely off guard. At an event, a woman around my age approached me with her mother, who was visibly emotional. She took my hands in hers, tears streaming down her cheeks, and said, 'I always wanted to be a dancer. But my family did not allow it. When I saw you singing on the show, something inside me cracked open. It felt like you were living the dream I never got to live.' What do you say in a moment like that? There was so much longing in her words, and also some strange, shared catharsis. To me, I had done something simple on screen. But for her, it had turned out to be profound.

Then there were the messages that told me I had made Delhi proud. These made my heart beat with joy. Because Delhi isn't just my city, it's also my root system. In some ways, that was one of the reasons I agreed to do the show in the first place: to give voice to a version of Delhi that is often misread or reduced to caricature. If I could embody even a fraction of its complexity, grace and quiet power, then that, to me, was reason enough.

What made the outpouring of love even more startling was how deeply it contrasted with what I had once feared. I remember telling my therapist, before the show aired, that people would probably see me as a spoiled brat—privileged and out of touch. But the response I received was something else entirely. Not only were people seeing me, they were feeling with me.

What I was experiencing wasn't just empathy, it was also fierce loyalty. If someone mocked a hairstyle I had sported or questioned a makeup choice, there would be fifty counter-comments from people I had never met. One person, for instance, criticized a certain pink eyeshadow—not knowing it had been dabbed on in a dark room, next to purple, which only looked pink under the studio lights. By morning, fans had spun the pink into a style statement, even linking it to the pink flamingos in the background. That's when I realized it wasn't just about how I looked. It was about who I was, or rather, who they saw in me.

There was something deeply moving in the fact that these strangers were offering me unconditional love. The grace with which people saw me and said, 'You are enough. Just as you are,' was very moving. I was reminded of how, when the show had come calling, people had warned me. 'You'll be exposing yourself to trolls', 'they'll judge your life choices', they had said. But I wasn't afraid. That was because I wasn't entering the show to be liked. Instead, I was entering to be seen as I am. And in doing that, I think I permitted others to do the same.

I remember Karan Johar once asked me if all the attention had made me arrogant. I smiled and said, 'No, I was always a little arrogant. But all this unconditional love? It's humbling me.' Truly, if anything, all that love made me even more conscious of the need to stay grounded, to fight whatever little arrogance may once have been there. To me, it felt like karma in motion. I had shown up as I was, and the universe had responded with grace.

Besides, being in the spotlight was never about personal glory. For me, it has always been the case of glamour for a cause. It is about amplifying the things I truly care about—art, aesthetics, culture and the quiet power of authenticity. I was never performing for the camera. If anything, I was reclaiming parts of myself.

'What about fame?' I am often asked. It came late, perhaps—but I wasn't waiting for it. In fact, I was already full. If anything, fame only added a microphone to a voice that was already singing. This is not to deny the fact that there are days when I wonder, what happens when the love fades? What happens when the DMs quiet down? But I know I am not in it for the applause. I am in it for the connection.

What the series ultimately reaffirmed for me is something I've always known. Fabulousness isn't a performance, it's a presence. It is also a love for life that radiates through the way that you take up space.

Chapter 5

Immersing in Creativity

I must have been all of twelve. I remember standing in a school corridor with paint-stained fingers, sketchbook in hand, having an animated conversation with my art teacher. In that moment, I felt . . . timeless, perhaps. I could not have known then that this quiet joy of creating would become my life's calling.

Creativity was never just a hobby for me. It felt like the very basis of my existence. My father painted quietly in his spare hours, even though he never called himself an artist. I remember watching his fingers intently as they glided across the canvas with confidence. There was a sense of immersion, of joy in him that left a strong imprint on me. Creativity, in fact, was never presented to me as something separate from life; it was life itself.

When I entered senior school, I was fortunate to study under Bishamber Khanna, a great artist and enamellist, whom I have spoken of before. He would invite me to join sessions with older students, saying, 'Come, I'm demonstrating a new technique today—you should be there.' He encouraged me to paint the same subject over and over—not to replicate it, but to truly understand it. For me, to be able to see beyond the surface. He also taught me how the same subject could be rendered in different media. I recall how he would say, 'Even a white sheet of paper, when folded, reveals a hundred shades.' It taught me that nothing is ever as flat or simple as it seems. Beauty reveals itself in layers, in angles, in shadows—if you are paying attention.

Those lessons shaped more than my art; they shaped my way of being. I learnt that to create anything meaningful, you must observe deeply and feel even more deeply.

Frequent encounters with artists like B.C. Sanyal and Manjit Bawa, who were friends of my teacher and often visited our art room, deepened that understanding. Just being in their presence, listening to their stories, watching them engage with art so intuitively left a lasting impression. Being around them taught me that art is not just what you make, it is how you radiate your intention.

The Artist Within

There have been times in my adult life when I disappeared into the act of making. Sans phones, sans noise—just my canvas, brush and sheer obsession.

At one point, painting consumed me with an urgency that felt almost primal. I set up a studio at home and began creating for hours—sometimes ten, twelve, even fourteen hours a day. I would wake up in the middle of the night with a vision and start sketching. Sometimes I would find myself staring at a blank canvas long after everyone else had gone to bed, my heart full.

For a while, it was intoxicating. I would lose myself in imagined scenes and paint them: I thought of a rainy afternoon in New York, snowfall in Gulmarg, the golden haze of sunset over Banaras, the sharp morning light across Rashtrapati Bhawan. I recall how, having worked non-stop for nearly ten months, my right leg went numb from the intensity of it all.

Eventually, I brought this deeply personal body of work together in an exhibition titled *Through My Eyes*, held at the India Habitat Centre. The show was inaugurated by the late Smt. Sheila Dikshit, then chief minister of Delhi, who graciously lit the ceremonial lamp. I sold every painting, keeping only one for myself. All the proceeds from the exhibition went to the Prime Minister's Relief Fund. Perhaps that is why the work carried so much energy, for it had been created for a cause larger than me. When the intention is pure, the art automatically becomes its own kind of catharsis.

But somewhere along the way, I also felt that I was burning myself out. Art, for me, has never been just about technique; it is about feeling, about energy. And what I was tapping into wasn't always light. There's a reason so many artists describe creativity as a kind of wound. Most people get hurt and move on. But artists? We tend to return to the ache. We keep scratching, keep digging—not to wallow, but to understand it, and then transform it into something beautiful on canvas. Think of poets who often tend to return to unrequited love, or filmmakers who craft entire worlds out of longing and loss. Artists often create not to escape the wound, but to make sense of it. It means going inward, peeling back layers, sitting with what hurts.

I knew that if I lived in that space too long, I would begin to disappear into it. That was when I decided I no longer wanted to make art from emptiness—not as a daily practice, and certainly not at the cost of my well-being .

These days, when I paint or photograph, it is to showcase heritage, to document architecture. I find myself returning to landscapes, to old buildings, to quiet moments. I still create but I protect my energy in the process.

Where Beauty Takes Shape

I have always needed my surroundings to speak to me. That is why when we built our home in Delhi, I approached it the way I approach art—intuitively, emotionally, even obsessively. I needed it to be a living archive of beauty, art, energy and emotion. It had to be a space where structure, art and design could live and breathe.

I took on the project with gusto, with the help of trained professionals, of course. I was involved in every aspect—from architectural planning and structural layout to visiting factories to source materials. I would attend site meetings during the day, review design plans, and spend nights sketching ideas or finalizing mood boards. Then there were constant calls with vendors across time zones, sometimes well past midnight. I immersed myself in the disciplines of architecture, lighting, landscaping, material sourcing and interiors. I learnt how to balance scale, rhythm and flow, not by following trends, but by following my intuition.

For me, building our home wasn't just about aesthetics; it was also about integrity. Every object, every curve, every finish had to speak. I wanted a powerful architecture to hold space for powerful art. I wanted walls that could breathe with artistic works, staircases that wouldn't interrupt a line of sight, and light that would let a sculpture or canvas speak for itself. One day, when I am older and my memory begins to fade, I want every corner to whisper its story to me. That was the kind of home I dreamed of—not just beautiful, but unforgettable. I had a vision in my head, and I was determined to bring it to life.

The process took nearly five years. By the time the house was completed, it had taught me more than I could have imagined. Alongside the feminine energy of aesthetics, the process also introduced me to the masculine energy of execution. But the intensity took its toll. I developed stomach ulcers from the stress. My sleep cycles were erratic. I was physically exhausted, but creatively alive.

What mattered most was that the home became exactly what I had envisioned—not just a place to live, but a quiet statement. A space that could hold art, beauty and life in a single, intentional breath. It was a matter of great pride that our home became the first Indian home to be featured in *Wallpaper* magazine, because of how closely art and interiors were intertwined. People from all over the world came to visit. I had designers and architects drawing inspiration. At the time, most interiors leaned towards minimalism. Our home shifted the conversation and suddenly, 'eclectic' became a buzzword.

I recall how I also received offers to start an interior design firm. I even took up a project or two, but quickly realized I am not a seller. I am a creator. I found it hard to translate my vision for someone else. So I let that chapter close. Of course, I still help friends do up their homes. But my own house remains the fullest expression of me—a space of art, energy and intention.

All of this is not to say that I didn't encounter my share of sceptics along the way. A friend, for instance, on visiting the house, remarked, 'All of Greater Kailash in Delhi was built by housewives.' I didn't quite know, at first, if it was meant as a compliment or as condescension. Was he looking down on housewives at large? Or on me? Either way, I chose not to react. It is my firm belief that not every action deserves a reaction. Not all people will understand your strength, and that is perfectly fine.

Collecting with Purpose

From the outside, our home is calm and unassuming, looking out over the greens of the Delhi Golf Club. But inside, every wall, every corner, carries a story. Paintings, tapestries, sculptures, mirrors collected lovingly over the years—placed not for display, but for dialogue. I gravitate towards pieces that stir something deep, that evoke emotion. Everything from seventeenth-century artefacts to contemporary installations flows in harmony, like a jigsaw puzzle coming together naturally. Visitors have returned multiple times and still maintain that they haven't been able to absorb everything.

Collecting, to me, is an openness to beauty in all its forms. This is why I don't separate 'Indian' from 'international', or 'contemporary' from 'classic'. You will find a Gio Ponti piece and a Riyas Komu sculpture, Marc Newson's *Lockheed Lounge* and Mrinalini Mukherjee's coiled hemp form. Because collecting, for me, is not about categories—it is about connections.

Collecting art is also my way of staying in conversation with the world. It's how I listen, how I express parts of myself that words can't always hold. In fact, I often say I don't collect art, I collect energy.

That said, I would also like to point out that while people often put collectors on a pedestal, I think collecting also comes from a place of deep yearning—maybe even deep insecurity. It is a deeply personal pursuit, a chase.

When something moves me, I go all in. I research its history, its technique. I approach each work as a fellow artist would. I grew up seeing these works in books and galleries, feeling something stir inside me. That curiosity never left me. I want to know where the artist was emotionally when they made it. What they saw, what they suffered, what they hoped for. And once the work is finally mine, the chase ends and a different relationship begins. It becomes part of my space. That is the joy of collecting.

The quiet magic of living with art is that it evolves just as you do, revealing new layers with time. That is why nothing in my home stays in the same place for too long. I rotate artworks often. This is not to impress anyone, but because I want them to keep speaking to me. Some pieces I've lived with for years still manage to surprise me. Like the works by Ram Kumar and Raza sahab, whose canvases seem to hum with memory, holding entire lifetimes within their brushstrokes.

Speaking of the legendary S.H. Raza, there is one episode etched in my memory forever. A moment that still brings goosebumps when I think of it. We had acquired one of his very important works. Sanjay is particular about provenance—and rightly so. So we decided to have the piece authenticated and took it to Raza sahab at the India International Centre in Delhi, where he was staying.

When he saw the painting, something completely unexpected happened. He sat down slowly, and his eyes started welling up. Then, to my utter shock, he began to sob. My heart dropped. I literally froze. A thousand thoughts raced through my mind—was it a fake? Had I made some terrible mistake?

Of course, I couldn't bring myself to say anything. He is so revered that I just could not ask him anything. Just being in his presence, one is rendered speechless.

After what felt like an eternity, he looked up. 'I am so grateful to you,' he said quietly. 'I haven't seen this painting in so many years. It's taken me back to the time I created it.' He paused, his voice thick with memory. 'I remember everything I poured into this work. I am so happy it's found its way to a collector like you.'

I was speechless. To hear those words was one of the most satisfying moments I have ever had as a collector.

Don't get me wrong—it was not because of the praise. But because of how much the artist himself was moved. That moment reminded me why I collect—not just for beauty or legacy, but to be a humble custodian of someone's deepest expression.

Then there are the works of M.F. Husain that evoke deep personal memories. Husain sahab was very close to my husband's family. When it was time for our wedding cards, they approached him with a request. Husain sahab had one condition. 'First, I'll meet the bride-to-be,' he said, 'and then I'll paint.'

When he met me, he smiled and declared, 'This is a Radha–Krishna *jodi*.' What followed was pure magic. He created four exquisite paintings, which were then printed and sent out as wedding invites. Each one was a masterpiece in its own right, bursting with love, colour, and Husain sahab's unmistakable energy. I have kept them safely ever since. To me, they are not just invitations; they are blessings. They are also a fond memory of being seen, truly seen, by a legend.

Championing Women Artists

I have always believed that women see the world differently. We tend to create from contradiction—from strength and softness, from logic and intuition. Nowhere is that more visible than in art.

When I began collecting, I found myself instinctively drawn to the work of women artists. Not out of tokenism or agenda, but because their pieces stirred something in me. At the risk of generalizing, I would like to say that I see a certain rawness, resilience and refusal to simplify the world.

Zarina Hashmi's minimalist work, for instance, speaks to me like poetry—full of silence and longing. Sheba Chhachhi's visual narratives, layered with memory and the feminine gaze, stay in my thoughts for days. Bharti Kher's bindi works—both intimate and monumental—feel like meditation. Anita Dube's explorations of the unsettling realities of our times have a pull I cannot turn away from. These aren't just works I admire; they are conversations I return to time and again.

I tend to draw strength from the work of women artists. When I see a woman taking risks with material or form, I see courage and fabulosity, and I want to do my bit to honour that.

Because when women artists thrive, culture shifts, narratives tend to shift.

Making Art Socially Happen

Not long after that seed-planting conversation with my guru in 2018—when he urged me to dedicate my life to service—I found myself asking: how do I serve through what I know best, through what moves me most deeply? The answer came intuitively. I wanted to build something that could spotlight creativity, nurture emerging voices and dissolve the walls that so often make art feel elite or exclusionary.

That's when I launched SPAF—the Shalini Passi Art Foundation—as an institutional commitment to nurturing the arts in deeper, quieter ways. The foundation offered a platform for artists to nurture multiple art forms, and among other things, supported exhibitions that challenge convention, discussions that spark dialogue, workshops that open up processes. But soon I realized something. With my name in the foundation's, SPAF carried a certain formality. I wanted to create something more fluid.

That's how MASH was born. If SPAF was the anchor, MASH became the wave—exploring the intersections of art, architecture, craft, design and fashion in an accessible, ever-evolving format. I was clear from the start: I didn't want to open yet another gallery. That would have been the easier route. What I envisioned was a not-for-profit space driven not by sales but by impact. A space where the return is not revenue, but resonance. A wave rippling outward—nurturing, uplifting, sparking something larger than itself.

I wanted a living, breathing, digital platform that made art feel alive, inclusive, conversational. Whether you are a twenty-something artist just out of college or someone flipping through Instagram in a quiet moment of the day, MASH is meant to stir something inside you. To make you pause, feel, connect.

It wasn't just about showcasing beauty. It was also about sparking dialogue and expanding the idea of what creativity could look like in everyday. From spotlighting emerging artists through monthly features to championing experimental voices across digital platforms, MASH became a way to amplify creative energy across disciplines. Our social channels also became living archives that curate updates on exhibitions, landmark auctions, cultural happenings from around the world.

The joy of discovering an artist is unlike anything else. It feels almost sacred. I still remember the first time I encountered the artist Narayan Biswas's work. There was a quiet power in it that stopped me in my tracks. His debut solo exhibition *Aitijhya* became more than just a show—it was a soulful excavation of India's architectural and cultural memory. Inspired by the *pol*—traditional clusters of homes where different castes and classes coexisted—his sculptural forms spoke volumes. Layering references to religion, politics and economy, he crafted towering structures that felt at once ancient and urgent. Each piece merged monumental fragments into a cohesive whole, creating a visual language that mirrored the complexity of our social fabric.

At MASH, we also nurture cross-disciplinary dialogues that push creative boundaries. One of our most joyful experiments in breaking silos was the *Fashion Wears Art* initiative. Curated as part of the Fashion Design Council of India (FDCI) x Lakmé Fashion Week, the project invited iconic Indian fashion designers and contemporary artists to come together—not to blend, but to spark something new.

We paired visionaries like J.J. Valaya with Waswo X Waswo, Rajesh Pratap Singh with Mithu Sen, Rohit Gandhi & Rahul Khanna with Vibha Galhotra, Varun Bahl with A. Ramachandran, Namrata Joshipura with Sudarshan Shetty, and Gautam Kalra with Siddharth Singh Bokolia—reimagining the runway as a moving gallery. This coalescence between art and fashion was symbolic of a dynamic, transformative space, offering a platform for artists and designers to push the envelope of creativity, challenge conventions and create unique, culturally significant works.

What unfolded wasn't just fashion, and it wasn't just art. It was—how do I describe it?—alchemy. It reaffirmed something I have always believed: when disciplines meet, something transcendent takes shape. *Fashion Wears Art* also echoed the cultural zeitgeist of our times, weaving together the imagery of contemporary art and fashion into a shared landscape.

Of course, we also envisaged the MASH Ball in support of UNICEF India—where art, glamour and giving converged. It was my way of turning a black-tie evening into something soulful. We raised funds for UNICEF's art-based therapy and early childhood development programs. But beyond the funds, what mattered was the message, that art can heal, elevate and transform lives—not just in theory, but tangibly.

MASH truly is my love letter to visibility, to belief, to the fierce, fabulous creativity that's just waiting to be witnessed.

Photography—Seeing with Devotion

All of this—the collecting, the curating, the championing—has always circled back to one truth for me: creativity is a sacred force. Whether I was holding space for other artists or disappearing into my own canvas, I have always believed that creating art is a form of meditation. In some seasons, that sacred act has taken the form of painting. In others, it has been photography calling out to me, offering me a new way to see, to hold, to honour what is fleeting.

I have never trained formally in photography. But I have always been an observer, perhaps even a keeper of silences. Sometimes, when words failed or felt too heavy, I found myself reaching for a camera. In fact, the first time I picked one up, it wasn't even mine but borrowed from a neighbour's daughter. What began as a small pursuit soon became something deeper. It became a practice of observation, a meditative effort, maybe even a way of worship.

During the pandemic, when the world shrank and suffering expanded, I felt an urgency to act. Of course, I wasn't a frontline worker, but I could still serve. I stepped out to deliver supplies, to support causes, and sometimes, simply to be present. I carried the camera with me almost instinctively, to help me bear witness to the city in its most fragile state.

Every day, I would set out, often as early as 4 a.m., going to one area at a time. The railway station, Red Fort, Connaught Place, Delhi Gate—places that usually brimmed with life, but were now hauntingly still. I made a conscious choice not to photograph people. My thought was simple: I did not want to turn someone else's vulnerability into an image. Instead, I captured empty streets, shuttered doors, abandoned bicycles, a faint *diya* flickering in the windowsill. Sometimes I would also shoot late into the night. My lens would fog up, my equipment would gather dust, but I would not relent. In all of this, light and shadow became my co-creators. I treated every shoot as if it might be my last. I wanted to give it everything. Not just to document Delhi, but to witness the haunting strength of a city that has withstood every tide.

Later, the idea for *Forever Delhi* was born—a series of black-and-white photographs that eventually became an exhibition I showcased at the *Architectural Digest* Fair in Mumbai, and later at the 2024 India Art Fair, presented through MASH. It was my tribute to the city I have lived in, loved in, learnt from. One hundred per cent of the proceeds from the show were donated to charity. Because if there is one thing Delhi has taught me, it is the power of continuity, of passing something on.

There was another city that kept tugging at my soul: Banaras. The spiritual axis of India; a place where the divine and the mundane blur so completely that the entire city feels like a theatre directed by the gods.

Not being technically trained in photography, my early photographs were clumsy, unfocused attempts. But something in the city called me back. This time, I wasn't trying to capture the city of Banaras in my camera. I wanted to listen and to let the city reveal itself to me. What I saw was not merely places or objects but witnesses of a belief system. I saw a realm where the boundaries between the divine and mortal blurred. I saw how the saffron robes of the sadhus weren't just an attire but instead reflected a deep spiritual intensity. Children dressed as gods crossed my path—a boy painted blue, embodying Shiva; a girl smiling gently, her forehead adorned with bindis like Parvati. In their play, I saw something deeper. I also witnessed how the Ganga didn't just flow—she held the devotion of millions. At the *aarti*, I felt a sense of being deeply held. Slowly but surely, I began to frame each shot the way a painter might compose a canvas. In all of this, nowhere was I chasing technical perfection. I was keen to capture the emotional truth, instead. I was grateful that through my lens, Banaras emerged not just as a city, but as a living embodiment of spirituality.

Photography, for me, isn't a performance. It is a way to re-spark fabulosity—through presence, through quiet awe. In a world filled with filters and spectacle, it is comforting to find solace in the stillness of my Nikon and Leica.

Through these frames, I also hope to remind others of something essential—that sometimes, the most fabulous thing you can do is notice, and then offer it back reverently.

Creativity as Sacred Ritual

People often ask me where it all comes from—the energy to create, to curate, to collect. The truth is that creativity isn't something I switch on and off. It is not a job title or a weekend hobby. For me, it is a way of being.

The line between art and life often blurs, bleeds into each other. That is why I choose the flowers that adorn my home like I choose my artworks, intuitively, with feeling. That is why my home is in a state of constant reinvention. A corner can change with the tilt of a sculpture, with the angle of the sun.

I believe that creativity, at its core, is about presence. Simply put, it is about paying attention. It is about bringing intention into the everyday—how you set a table, how you arrange a shelf, how you style your hair, how you take a photograph that maybe no one will even see.

It's also about devotion. Let me clarify. I do not mean that in a solemn, heavy sense. I mean it as reverence for beauty, for texture, rhythm, harmony. It is that act of transformation—when a blank wall becomes a gallery, when a mundane moment becomes a memory.

That is what art or any other form of creativity does. It turns the ordinary into the sacred, the personal into the universal.

Re-sparking Fabulosity—A Love Note to the Reader

I believe you do not have to be a painter, a sculptor or a collector to live artfully. You just have to notice more.

Observe the way the light shifts. Notice your breath when you are dancing. Pay attention to the rhythm, not always the lyrics. Curate your space like it matters—not for Instagram, but for your spirit. Make something with your hands. Simply rearrange your books or write a letter or just draw with your children. Go ahead and stitch a patch onto something worn. See the poetry that exists not in seemingly perfect pieces but also broken ones—the chipped ceramics, the wilted flowers, those faded photographs. Let creativity be your compass. Sometimes we see creativity as an escape from life but look at it as a way to meet life with even more wonder.

Importantly, creativity and fabulosity isn't about having everything figured out. It is about staying awake to possibilities—to beauty, to feeling, to the divinity that lives inside the ordinary.

Chapter 6

The Art of Giving

There was a moment in my life when I was feeling full, but not truly fulfilled. A lot was going for me, yet something within stirred quietly but insistently. I began asking myself if *there is something more I am meant to do with this life*.

I have spoken about this moment before, and perhaps that's only fitting. I find myself circling back to it often because that one moment shifted something in me, giving me both purpose and direction. This is the time I turned to my Guru with the question that had been quietly stirring within me: *What should I do with this energy, this access, this awareness?* I asked. His reply was steady, almost serene. *Use what you've been given to serve, he said.*

That conversation was life-changing. It reframed my entire understanding of giving. I realized how giving wasn't about occasional acts of charity—I had been doing that for years anyway. It was about becoming a conduit and letting intention and compassion flow through me. If one has to re-spark one's life, to reignite purpose, joy and connection, there is no better place to begin than with giving.

It is not that I had to be taught the spirit of giving. I had grown up witnessing generosity in quiet, instinctive acts embedded in the everyday rituals of our lives. One of my early memories is of my grandfather giving away a beautiful home in Jor Bagh, one of Delhi's most sought-after neighbourhoods, because his younger brother's family had asked for it. It was a simple, open-hearted *yes*, one that left no room for negotiation or even second thoughts. My grandmother had the same instinctive grace. I saw her quietly part with pieces of her jewellery when someone reached out for help. I never heard my mother use words like 'social service', yet I always remember her making thoughtful gestures that added up to a life of deep kindness.

Without realizing it, I had internalized that inner compass. I never felt that giving was a duty or some moral checkbox to be ticked. To me, it simply felt like the most natural thing to do. Years later, when I had the calling to make an offering of my jewellery at Tirupati Balaji, I was reminded of the quiet legacy I carry. That act not only felt deeply personal, it almost felt like muscle memory passed down through generations.

That legacy of giving didn't just stay within the walls of our home—it also travelled with me wherever I went, into classrooms and community drives. In school, we were encouraged to look beyond ourselves. We were encouraged not only to donate toys and clothes, we were also taught to volunteer our time and participate in programmes that introduced us to the idea of service. Those early moments taught me that giving isn't about the size of your contribution, it is about the difference it creates in someone else's life.

As I grew and my worldview expanded, stories of people like Mother Teresa and global philanthropists like the Rockefellers shaped my understanding of generosity. But perhaps the most enduring influence on me has been Ratan Tata—not just as an icon from afar, but as someone I saw up close, he being a family friend.

I remember, when my son was very young—perhaps five or six—he would climb onto Ratan Uncle's lap and innocently declare, 'You look like Indiana Jones!' He had just watched *Raiders of the Lost Ark* and, with childlike innocence, decided that Mr Tata bore a striking resemblance to Harrison Ford. Ratan Uncle blushed on hearing him and responded with his characteristic warmth and grace.

I once remember suffering a severe skin burn while swimming in Bali in the late 1990s. The sun had come out after days of rain, and I hadn't realized how harsh it had become. The damage to my skin was extensive. Ratan Uncle not only advised me on which doctors to see but also came to visit me at home. That moment—of someone so powerful, so busy, taking the time to check in with genuine care—was heart-warming. That is the man he was: a man of enormous influence who lived with such simplicity and humility. He often drove himself, ate modestly, and showed kindness in every gesture. I distinctly remember how he would always pause to make eye contact with someone serving him, nodding in acknowledgement. There was no inflated self-importance, just quiet dignity. Watching him over the years taught me that power and humility are not opposites, and that true influence never needs to announce itself.

What also deepened my relationship with giving was motherhood. It brought out a strength I had not fully recognized until then. I found in myself an emotional resilience, a deeper empathy. It was as if my heart had cracked open—in the best possible way, of course. It ensured that I was even more attuned to the struggles of others, more affected by their pain and far more compelled to act.

Giving, for me, has never been about guilt or obligation. Instead, it has always come from a place of fullness. I don't really believe in making a self-sacrifice that empties you out. Real and sustained giving happens when you are deeply rooted in yourself. When you are content, aligned and aware, you can give.

Over the years, I have also realized that generosity isn't just something you express outwardly. It is the quality of listening, of showing up. Sometimes, writing a cheque is the easiest thing to do, if you have the resources. But giving your time, your attention, your emotional energy? That takes far more. Perhaps that's why I am drawn to the word 'flow' when I speak of philanthropy. Because for me, giving is not about fixed hierarchies. It is not just the privileged giving to the underprivileged, or the fortunate helping the less fortunate. I may offer something that uplifts someone, but what I receive in return is equally profound.

That is the paradox of giving. You think you are offering something to someone else, and yet in the process, you become fuller yourself.

But over time, I have also realized that while giving from the heart is beautiful, it can also be demanding. Especially when you are a deeply emotional person like me. Presence isn't always easy, and connection need not always be light. Sometimes, the kindest thing you can do, for yourself and for others is to know your limits. I learnt this lesson the hard way, while I was still in school. I still remember that we had a program that encouraged us to teach underprivileged children. I was paired with a younger girl, a special-needs student, who very quickly became deeply attached to me. She would only respond to me, only listen when I taught her. She adored me, perhaps because I was gentle with her, or maybe because she liked how I looked or spoke. It was a sweet bond, one that grew quickly.

But one Monday, after I had missed teaching her over the weekend, I walked into class to find her in distress. Without warning, she bit me. I was still a child myself, maybe in the eighth or ninth grade, and I didn't quite know how to process fully what had just happened. I knew, though, that she did that not hurt me out of malice, but out of sheer emotional overwhelm.

That moment, however, shook something inside me. Not because I blamed her, of course, I didn't. What I came to realize, though, was that there is an emotional weight that comes with human connection. As someone who feels deeply, I realized I could not immerse myself in individual stories where I could not offer permanence. Over time, I have learnt to honour that about myself. Even today, I don't visit hospitals or attend funerals not out of avoidance, but because those spaces stay with me too deeply.

What that incident taught me is the importance of boundaries. When I speak of boundaries, it is not in the context of withholding, but as a means of sustaining oneself. The question to ask yourself is, how can I give meaningfully without depleting myself? How do I support others in a way that does not leave both of us hurting when I cannot show up? I realized that the most effective philanthropy, at least for me, is the kind that creates a structure, as opposed to one that relies on one-on-one emotional immersion. It is not because I don't care, but precisely because I care too much. This is exactly why I'm deliberate about how I give. I do not want to be tied down in ways that drain me. Instead, I want to give in ways that uplift, that flow. In fact, it is something I apply not only to philanthropy, but also to life. I have come to realize that the fewer expectations others have of me, the freer I am to show up fully, without resentment. That way, if I am truly there, it is because I want to be, not because I am bound to be.

But just because I've chosen not to immerse myself emotionally in every situation, it doesn't mean I am closed to intimacy or responsibility. In fact, some moments come into your life as callings, and you instinctively know that *this one, I have to answer*. One such moment came when our home was being constructed. This elderly carpenter was working on the site, someone who had done small jobs for us for years. We did not know much about his life, though. He was just always around, dependable and quiet. Towards the end of the project, he sadly passed away in an accident. Only then did we learn that he had been raising two grandchildren on his own. His son had died, and his daughter-in-law had remarried and left the children in his care. Since then, he, with his aging body and limited resources, had been silently holding their world together.

My husband didn't hesitate for a second on hearing about the children. He didn't just write a cheque, he adopted the children, put them in boarding school and took full responsibility for their upbringing. He visited their school, checked on them like a parent would. To me, that is what true generosity looks like. It is not always planned. Sometimes it is just an instinctive yes to a situation that presents itself without any warning.

A Ball with a Soul

Over the years, that sense of surrender began to shape not just how I gave, but also what I created. My association with UNICEF was the beginning of something much deeper. It became a way to channel both creativity and compassion into a shared vision for impact. As an organization, their work aligned with the causes I cared about—children's rights, emotional healing, education, dignity. Their Early Childhood Development and Art-Based Therapy initiatives struck a personal chord. These weren't abstract programmes but on-ground efforts changing real lives. It was about helping children recover from trauma, giving caregivers the tools to nurture with compassion, and placing emotional well-being at the heart of development.

Today, any fee I receive from my creative assignments—whether for a shoot, an appearance, or my fee for the Netflix series—goes directly to UNICEF. Supporting these causes feels like a responsibility, one I am ready to honour not just with funds, but with creativity and conviction. That's how the idea for the MASH Ball in support of UNICEF India was born, something I have alluded to before.

I didn't want it to be just another charity gala. I wanted it to bring together people from different walks of life, to build a sense of community among artists, donors, dreamers and doers. The proceeds were directed to UNICEF's Art-Based Therapy programme, which uses creative expression as a tool for healing and emotional recovery, and to the Early Childhood Development initiative, which empowers caregivers, strengthens community systems and supports children during their most formative years.

Art, for me, has always been more than an aesthetic. It is a language, a way to tell enduring stories. That is why I was particularly drawn to the idea of using art as therapy for children living in stress and conflict. There is something deeply powerful about turning pain into colour, fear into form. I believe art can hold space like little else.

The Ball itself was a reflection of this belief. It was glamorous, but equally grounded. The whole energy was electric. It reminded me that fabulousness, at its best, is generous. It sparks something larger than itself; it opens doors and builds bridges. We often underestimate how much influence we carry as individuals, as communities, as creators. The MASH Ball was my way of reminding myself and others, that giving can be joyful. It can be luminous. It can absolutely be fabulous.

People often ask me, 'But did it raise funds?' Of course it did. But most importantly, it raised energy. Transformation begins with an emotional shift, and at the Ball, that shift was palpable. I saw how deeply people connected with the cause. That, to me, is the future of philanthropy—not an obligation, but an invitation.

Purnia—Grace at the Grassroots

When I began my collaboration with UNICEF, it was because their philosophy resonated with my own. It was important to me that they weren't simply delivering aid, they were also building capacity. Most importantly, they were embedding themselves within communities to create long-term change. I loved the multidimensional approach, grounded in humility and partnership.

But nothing compared to seeing that work in action.

My visit to Purnia in Bihar was one of the most grounding, illuminating experiences of my life. What was most uplifting was that what I saw wasn't despair; it was quiet resilience, dignity, resourcefulness in its most unadorned form.

Through a partnership between UNICEF, the state government, and catalytic support from my foundation, we had been developing a Responsive Ecosystem for Early Childhood Development in the aspirational districts of Baisi in Purnia and Palasi in Araria. The goal has always been long-term—training frontline workers, empowering caregivers, strengthening systems and building trust at the grassroots.

This was when I saw firsthand the resilience of families and children growing up in incredibly difficult conditions. I was struck by how untrue many of the stereotypes about rural India really are. I saw young mothers, holding babies in their arms, listening with fierce attentiveness to conversations on health, nutrition and hygiene. Some asked questions with quiet confidence. What also moved me was the presence of family members beside them. They were not just passively accompanying, but encouraging them, willing them to succeed. They understood that when a mother thrives, so does her child. These glimpses stayed with me. They reminded me that aspirations don't belong to a single postcode. They exist wherever people are given even a small chance to rise.

Then there were the small things that linger in your heart. It was heartwarming to see how children found joy in the simplest things, turning scraps and discarded bits into toys, for instance. You could hear children singing, laughter echoing through the rooms. Caregivers and educators were sitting on the floor, simply being present. There wasn't any trace of hierarchy or formality. It was just a deep sense of trust and of human connection. I was reminded that the most powerful lessons come from the lived intelligence of people who know how to make the most of very little. What struck me the most, though, was that no one here wanted pity or even charity. They were asking for access, for opportunity and respect.

Strangely, the incident took me back several years and reminded me of my early days back in school, when I was teaching a young special-needs student. I recalled how emotionally intense that connection had been. But what I was seeing here was different. Here was a structure of care, not dependency. That difference mattered deeply to me.

When I left Purnia, I carried many learnings back with me. Among them, a kind of clarity: that the most fabulous thing you can sometimes do is sit beside someone in their struggle and truly listen.

The Art of Inspiring Others

I have always believed that inspiration is also a form of giving. When someone shows you what is possible through their ideas, their courage, or their commitment, they hand you a torch, or should I say a mirror, that reflects your own potential.

That is what I felt when I saw Mira Nair being honoured at the Better World Fund's programme at Cannes. What is truly fabulous is how she has used her artistry for advocacy. From the much-celebrated film, *Salaam Bombay* to the Salaam Baalak Trust, she has created more than cinema, in fact, she has created real change. Her film gave a voice to street children, and the trust she helped establish continues to protect and empower them decades later.

The Global Gift Gala was yet another eye-opener for me. Co-hosted by Eva Longoria and Maria Bravo, that event was a great blend of elegance with empathy. I strongly believe that events such as these aren't just fundraisers; they build a whole emotional landscape. I saw guests committing themselves to the vision of a better world. When philanthropy meets storytelling, when artistic expression meets genuine impact, that is the kind of magic that happens, and I was fortunate to witness it. It reminded me that true giving requires both soul and structure; it requires sincerity and also strategy. It is heartening for me to also know that, among other projects, The Global Gift Foundation supports Harmony House, an NGO dedicated to rescuing homeless children, closer home, in Gurgaon.

All of this also made me wonder, how do we build more of that kind of energy around causes in India? How do we ensure that people feel deeply connected, both emotionally and financially, to the impact they are helping create?

That question has stayed with me as I envision newer editions of the MASH Ball. I know that every choice we make needs to be about stirring hearts. I don't claim to have all the answers. But I do know that when giving is infused with creativity, humility and joy, it becomes contagious.

That to me, is the future of fabulous philanthropy. Because true fabulousness is about what you stand for. It's about turning your light outward.

Chapter 7

Bonds of a Lifetime

Clamshells in the Ocean

While on a family holiday in the Maldives, we decided to scuba dive. Before we knew it, we were surrounded by coral reefs and schools of fish. Every now and then, we were enthralled by a reef shark that passed us by in the distance. If it felt like a totally surreal experience, there was more to come. Suddenly, we saw giant clams in vivid colours, slowly opening and closing, releasing soft bursts of bubbles around them. It felt like a hidden world was revealing itself to us.

When we came up to the surface, I must have spoken with such fascination that Robin, who was perhaps just six at the time, made it his mission to find me a clamshell. He went searching along the beach for hours, patient and determined in the way only children can be. Suddenly, I heard him calling out: 'Mom! I've found it! It's too big for me to carry!' When I ran towards him, sure enough, he had spotted a shell in the shallow waters. Having found it, he didn't want to move, afraid he would lose the exact spot.

Together, we pulled out that enormous clamshell. That moment, when we were laughing with joy as if we had found a treasure, is etched in my memory. I distinctively recall how proud he looked, standing there with his hair tousled by the sea breeze, holding this thing that had become a shared treasure for both of us.

That incident reminded me that while we often speak of fabulousness as an individual pursuit, the real sparkle lies in the people who light you up. It is these bonds that make everything more vivid. Whether it is love, family, friends or collaborators, no one can be truly fabulous alone.

My Inner Circle

For me, the foundation of everything I am begins at home, with the people whose presence is woven into my earliest memories. My inner circle isn't just close; it is where I begin and return.

My grandmother was the most powerful presence in my life. I loved that she was deeply spiritual, selfless, and utterly detached from worldly affairs. 'Live in the world, but don't be of it,' she often said. It is a line that has gone on to shape my own relationship with society.

She was fiercely protective in her own gentle way. I remember once, when both my parents and grandparents had to step out for unavoidable work, she didn't want to leave me alone at home with the staff. So she asked my uncle, who was then studying at IIT, to skip his classes and stay with me. Her love was that fierce, that focused. What is also etched in my memory is the time when I once fell ill as a child, and she quietly took a vow to turn vegetarian for the rest of her life. There was no fanfare, no announcement from her of having made a big sacrifice. It was pure love expressed through quiet sacrifice. That kind of love stays with you. It wraps itself around your spirit long after the person is gone.

Years later, when she developed a brain tumour, I was devastated. Somewhere deep within, I have always felt it was karmically linked. That all her quiet love, all those unspoken vows, had found their way into her body. I can still feel in my bones the panic that had gripped me the day she stepped out for her usual walk and didn't return. Hours passed; it was pouring hard. We set out to look for her. We searched everywhere, hearts in our mouths. When we finally found her, soaked and disoriented, I knew something had changed. From then on, her health declined. That year was incredibly tough for me. I was not just watching her fade, but I was also struggling with my own health. I felt cracked open, physically and emotionally, as if I couldn't carry the weight of the loss.

But her spirit never left me. Her calm detachment, her quiet discipline, the way she remained untouched by noise or drama—all of it became a part of me. She truly lived in the world, but wasn't of it. In my own way, I try to carry that forward.

While my grandmother taught me stillness, my mother showed me movement. A classic Virgo, she is hardworking, affectionate, quietly formidable. An incredible cook and a devoted homemaker, she pours her energy into nurturing those around her. I have always seen her hold the fort, no matter what storms shook us.

Her only complaint with me these days? 'Your sister calls me five times a day,' she says with mock exasperation. 'As for you, even if there is any crisis, I have to hear about it from Robin or your staff.' But that is just who I am. I would rather quietly take care of things than worry anyone. Perhaps it is simply my way of protecting the people I love.

If my mother is the nurturer, my father gives me structure and strength. Their energies are different, but complementary. He is an artist in his own right—not a trained architect, but someone with an instinctive understanding of space, stone and wood. The details of architecture, the grain of good furniture, the balance in finishes—I absorbed all of that from watching him. Growing up, I was average at studies, and he would often make me write this one sentence—'Practice makes a man perfect'—over and over again. At the time, I didn't fully understand its purpose. Now I do. In fact, that repetition, that discipline, is a part of my DNA now. At a restaurant once, I remember a chef asking him, 'How's the dish?' His reply was so characteristic: 'If it was good, I would've told you,' He said nonchalantly. That is his style—precise, unsparing and clear. From him, I learnt that authority is elegant when it comes without ego. He carries that quiet command, and it shaped the way I carry myself today.

The one who has been my anchor, my mirror, my still point in a turning world, is Sanjay. There are moments when he has felt like a parent, at others my fiercest critic, and always my cheerleader. We got married very young, but never once did I feel the need to shrink myself to fit into his frame. With Sanjay, I could grow. I could stumble, stretch, evolve, knowing he would honour that.

Come to think of it, we are different in the most fundamental ways. Sanjay is precise and methodical. He identifies every goal clearly and moves towards it with unwavering discipline. I, on the other hand, am led by instinct. I will pour my heart into something seemingly small, overlook the big, and then circle back with a burst of clarity. My rhythm is unpredictable, emotional. His is focused, steady. What binds us is our shared work ethic, our belief in building something meaningful, and our commitment to giving back.

What I love most about him is how deeply connected he is—to his family, to mine, to everyone in our lives. He calls my parents twice a day, checks in on our friends, stays in touch with extended family. He shows up in the most consistent, caring ways. I am different—I retreat more and tend to savour my solitude.

When we travel, we share a common thirst for discovery—skiing, diving, exploring. But come to think of it, even there, our styles differ. I will lose myself in an art gallery, while Sanjay steps out mid-visit to make work calls or even to solve someone's problem. I still remember the time we were halfway up Mont Blanc, and there he was on the phone, helping someone navigate a crisis. That is him, grounded and available, even when scaling a mountain.

Our complementary natures are also revealed in the way we give. Sanjay responds instantly—if there is a flood, a tragedy, he doesn't wait. He simply acts. I, in contrast, like to build systems. I think in terms of long arcs. But our hearts, I believe, are in the same place.

For as long as I can remember, we have been building together, debating decisions, weighing possibilities. I will walk into a space and tell him if I feel the energy is right. I cannot explain it, but he trusts it. Just as I trust his judgement and his calm clarity in the face of complexity. All I can say is that together, we have found a rhythm that works. Not because we are alike, but because we listen, respect, and give each other room to be who we are.

People often ask what makes a relationship fabulous. For me, the answer is simple: alignment of energy. You don't need someone to be exactly like you. What you do need is someone who moves through life with equal intensity. Sanjay and I are that team. Together, we have built, failed, rebuilt, and kept going. That, to me, defines intimacy, the everyday companionship of effort and intention.

Robin, our son, has grown up watching this dance. He has absorbed the values of respect and resilience that we have modelled. And while I don't speak much about him publicly, I will say that being his mother has been one of the most profound roles of my life. It has made me softer and stronger at the same time.

Perhaps that is what the deepest relationships do—they shape you in subtle but enduring ways. The most powerful ones are built in small, continuous acts of showing up. That is also the circle I cherish, the one that sees me fully and holds space for me, every time.

Chosen Bonds

Of course, not every bond is written in blood. Some are bonds you choose, and yet they etch themselves quietly into your soul.

Such people come with quiet loyalty. They come with the instinct to check in at just the right moment. They also come with the grace not to disappear when the spotlight moves elsewhere.

While in school, I remember moments when others hesitated to include someone in the group simply because they weren't part of the 'right' crowd. But I didn't care about such things. If you were kind to me, if we could laugh over silly things, if there was a spark of connection, I would stand by you. I have never understood the instinct to distance yourself from people just because they are going through a hard time. If anything, isn't that when they need you most?

That belief has followed me into adulthood. There have been times when I have heard people say, 'Don't invite her, she's not relevant anymore,' or, 'He doesn't fit the vibe.' But I have never believed in that kind of thinking. Friendship to me isn't PR. You don't unfriend someone because they are not trending. Wealth can come and go. But character, how you stand by people, that stays. I believe I am too old school to have seasonal friendships.

Over the years, I've found quiet ways to show up for my friends. Calling to check in when I sensed something was not right. I have stood up for people when others spoke poorly of them, calmly saying, 'Please don't say that in front of me.' What is interesting is that even the person gossiping knows that if they were in trouble, I would be there for them too. That is the respect that consistency earns you. And along the way, what I have also learnt is that standing by people does not just help them, it also empowers you.

Come to think of it, I have even had acquaintances, women I am not particularly close to, call me during major life decisions. 'I am going through a rough patch,' they'll say. 'I haven't told anyone, but I need your advice.' Why me, I have often asked myself. The answer I always get is that they know I won't gossip or judge. What I will do instead is simply listen and hold it sacred. That kind of trust isn't built in a day. It is earned over years of knowing when to show up and when to stay silent.

I saw a living example of this when my grandmother would refuse to attend women's gatherings where the talk turned petty. 'They just talk ill about their daughters-in-law,' she would say, choosing instead to protect her peace. I think I have inherited this streak from her. That quiet strength, that refusal to partake in bitterness—that was her gift to me. I have no appetite for tearing people down. If the energy isn't elevating, I would rather be alone.

I have even had people come up to me in professional settings with things they cannot say elsewhere. 'You will understand,' they say. The more I think about it, the more I realize it isn't because I always have the perfect solution, but because I listen without trying to fix them. I don't weaponize their vulnerability. I know how deeply it cuts when someone you trust turns your truth into currency. I can never be that person, someone who is a transaction disguised as a friend. In fact, some of the most meaningful relationships in my life have been built on the unspoken agreement that your truth is safe with me.

And yet, there is one stereotype I encounter time and again: that people in public life cannot truly be friends. Most assume that underneath the smiles, it's all competition. But that hasn't been my experience. I have had friendships that span both the glamorous and the grounded, and both have been equally enduring. In either space, I value the same things—trust, shared values, and the freedom to be completely real. One of my longest-standing friendships is with Gauri Khan, who embodies grace and balance. We have known each other for over three decades. Shah Rukh and Sanjay were at school together, and over time, we built a quiet, enduring bond. While we are different as people—she more measured, I more instinctive—we always hold space for each other. That, to me, is what connection is really about.

Another dear friend who has stood by me with similar grace is Manish Malhotra. For someone who juggles the biggest shows and projects in the world of fashion, Manish has a rare quality: he always shows up. He may be occupied with a major event, but will still call to ask, 'What are you wearing?' Somehow, no matter how busy, he'll help style you to perfection. Beyond the glamour is an incredibly hardworking, thoughtful person who is genuinely good at nurturing relationships.

To me, that's what being fabulous truly means. It isn't just about sharing the front row at fashion week. It is also about bringing soup when someone is down. It is telling a friend the truth with kindness. It is lifting each other up, without needing credit or applause.

Lifting as We Climb

People often ask if I mentor younger women. I do, though it may not always be in structured, formal ways. Sometimes it is a quiet nudge. Sometimes a late-night conversation. At others, it is simply holding space for someone overwhelmed who needs to hear that this too shall pass, that she isn't crazy or weak.

There have been many moments when I have looked at a younger girl—someone in college, or just starting her creative journey—and felt I was seeing a version of myself. She may be shy, a little unsure, too honest for her own good, too upright to play games. I find myself telling her gently, 'Don't let the world harden you. Don't dilute your light to fit in.' I know what it feels like to wonder if your softness is a flaw. I promise them it isn't.

Over the years, I have been fortunate to work with many women, designers, architects, even young interns who remind me why I do what I do. I feel that their spark reignites mine. In fact, some of my deepest kinships have been born not in drawing rooms, but in studios, in moments of shared curiosity, while co-creating something that didn't exist the moment before. When you find the right people, I have always found that magic happens. Many of the young women I've supported through my foundation also started out as collaborators. I wasn't thinking of mentoring them formally. But then a moment of recognition flickers, and you find yourself saying, 'Don't lose your fire.'

At the end of the day, mentorship isn't about control or credit. It is about belief. It is telling someone, 'You've got this. And if you fall, I'm here.' In my experience, the best mentorship offers presence and consistency.

That belief has shaped the way I have kept my circle small and sacred. There is one important caveat, though. A small and sacred circle isn't a group of people who agree with everything you say. In fact, if you decide to surround yourself with *chamchas*, yes-men or yes-women, you tend to lose touch with reality. Your energy stagnates because nothing comes to you unfiltered; it's all being relayed through someone else's lens, someone else's motives and someone else's insecurities. I have seen people travel with such yes-men who tell them where to dine, accompany them everywhere and curate their lives down to the last detail. These people act as human shields, deciding who gets access and who doesn't. The fact, however, is that the moment you let people hover around you, micromanaging your social calendar, running every small errand, feeding you gossip, you stop experiencing life directly.

To my mind, the alternative is far more empowering—to learn to do things yourself. Book your own travel, plan your own itineraries, research your own hotels, handle your own communication, design your own clothes or jewellery if that excites you, dive into architecture, lighting, textiles, carpets, interiors—whatever your life brings you into contact with. You may not be an expert in every field, but you can certainly develop breadth and a kind of inner knowing that only comes from curiosity. This has been my philosophy ever since I was in school. Whenever I wanted to understand something, I went to a class, bought a book, or found a teacher. I have always preferred learning over outsourcing and that habit has shaped my entire worldview. When you stay inquisitive, your life becomes a long, thrilling apprenticeship. You begin to connect the dots, knowledge from one field informs another, and your instincts sharpen. Of course, when you truly need help, you need to find the best people in the field and collaborate with them. There is a big difference between hiring someone for their expertise and having a coterie of hangers-on whose only role is to orbit you. In my opinion, life is too rich to live through middlemen. True fabulousness can thrive in environments where everyone stands tall, where conversations flow freely, and where people come together because they genuinely care, not because there is power to gain.

In fact, I believe deeply in the power of feminine energy. Women can be each other's fiercest protectors. My team is almost entirely women too—strong, intuitive, sharp. There is something unspoken between us, a current of mutual respect, of trust, of having each other's backs.

Through MASH and my art foundation, I have supported many women artists. Some I have collected, others I have platformed. All I have believed in. Because I know how hard it can be to have your voice heard in a room never designed for you.

But let me be honest: talking about women's issues stirs something raw in me. Sometimes it makes me feel helpless, angry. At other times, it makes me want to change everything overnight. But change, I understand, needs more than emotion. It needs infrastructure, policy, institutional will. Most importantly, real impact requires change to seep into the fabric of society.

We live in a society full of contradictions. Women are more educated than ever before. They are brilliant students, yet their brilliance is often boxed in by outdated expectations. Many still lack professional experience and financial independence. Marriages still happen early; divorce and widowhood remain taboo. Domestic violence continues, often unspoken, behind closed doors.

Even for those who navigate these structural constraints, there are several other quiet forces that they need to contend with. Take ageism, for instance. It shows up in more ways than one. In advertising, where twenty-year-olds are seen advocating beauty products to women twice their age, as if ageing is something to conceal. It is also seen in the way we define success through glossy lists like *30 Under 30* or *40 Under 40*, as if your worth has a countdown.

But what about the women who stepped away to raise a family? The ones restarting their careers in their late 30s or 40s? Where is the recognition for them? These are women who are audaciously learning new systems, who are navigating outdated hierarchies, and most importantly, who are rebuilding their confidence. Yet the world barely acknowledges their return. Why aren't there awards for the kind of strength it takes to re-enter a fast-moving corporate world after a fifteen-year break? For adapting to new technologies, re-establishing a professional identity, and starting courageously all over again?

While we maintain that we care about empowerment, the fact is that it plays better on a panel than in policy. For starters, it is important that we call out the disconnect between what we applaud in public and what we enable in private.

I cannot remind young women enough that financial independence is not just about money, it's also about self-respect. Just as I challenge this idea that housewives 'do nothing'. I know how hard that job is. I have lived some version of it, and I honour it. I often say this: if you are a woman doubting yourself, whisper this into your soul: *You are a goddess. You are Durga, Kali, Lakshmi, Saraswati, Parvati*, each representing a different aspect of Shakti's power. You can hold the world in your hands and still keep your heart intact. You don't need to shout to be powerful. Just stay true. The world always comes around.

Because Fabulousness Is Contagious

Over time, I've come to realize that fabulousness is a shared vibration. One where you don't just flourish yourself, you help others rise too.

As for the most fabulous thing you can do in any relationship? It is simply to be fully present. You need not be flawless; all you need to be is honest, grounded, and real. Despite your best intentions, some relationships will uplift you, while others will teach you through pain. But each one, in its own way, will shape you. I can say that I have learnt from every single person that I have ever come across. Every person leaves behind something. Sometimes it may be an inspiration, at other times a warning. Even those I disagreed with, have been my teachers. They showed me who I didn't want to become, how I didn't want to react. That too, is a gift.

Fabulousness, to me, is also not about winning every relationship. Instead, it is about moving through them with grace and integrity. Equally, it is also about having the clarity to walk away when needed and having enough strength to stay when it matters.

Chapter 8

Living Between Worlds

Some people find their lane early; they take pride in having a fixed identity, a single aesthetic, one worldview. But that was never my path. For as long as I can remember, I have always lived between worlds—between tradition and modernity, between high art and everyday craft, between the local and the global, or between red-carpet glamour and deeply private rituals. I have always moved fluidly between them, and unapologetically.

I didn't just move through these spaces; I also found joy in connecting them. Over the years, I have come to see that fabulousness is often about letting different energies pass through you, while still staying centred.

Curiously, I think it is Delhi that trained me to live like this. It taught me to hold contradictions without flinching. I believe Delhi is a city of layers. You can turn one corner and land in an age-old temple and turn another to walk into an international art gallery. One minute you might step out to pick up flowers from the market for a *pooja*, and an hour later be dressed in couture for a fashion event. My own childhood moved through those layers. I grew up in a home steeped in tradition, while outside the city buzzed with modernity, ambition and reinvention. I loved both these worlds, and interestingly, I never felt the need to choose between them.

Growing up in Delhi, I was also surrounded by spaces where art was truly lived. Places like Triveni Kala Sangam and Lalit Kala Akademi weren't just distant institutions; they felt like an intrinsic part of the city's rhythm. In Delhi, culture wasn't something we needed to schedule, it was all around us, all the time. I remember how excited I would be each time I received a new pamphlet announcing a cultural event, a performance, or a new show. For the young me, the city felt alive, full of possibility.

While art throbbed in the city's cultural veins, the city itself was on the move. In fact, the '80s and early '90s were transformative years for Delhi. For one, the Asian Games changed the city's skyline. A wave of new apartment complexes and stadiums redefined its urban identity. I recall visiting a friend living in one of the early high-rises. To my young self, it felt like stepping into the future. It was my first glimpse of how space could shape identity. It made me see that architecture was not just about new buildings, but also about possibility. There was a sense of movement, of progress in the very air. Importantly, I also saw how a city could expand and yet not forget its roots. To my young mind, that became an early blueprint.

That idea that you could grow without losing your essence echoed in other aspects of my life too. In school, we were encouraged to try various things, and nobody told us to stay in our lane. Even if your only role in the school play was to stand quietly as a tree, you stood there as the best tree ever. That experience taught me the value of presence. You didn't necessarily have to lead to belong, but you did have to show up.

I remember a school sports event where I was involved in multiple activities. At one point, the teacher told me to step back, perhaps to give others a chance. While I did that, I also made sure that at every rehearsal, I showed up fully, with presence and focus. By the end, the teacher had asked me to move ahead in the queue, not because I had asked, but because I had quietly claimed my position.

Another moment from school still makes me smile. We didn't have a hockey team, but one day our sports teacher walked up to a group of us who participated in athletics and said, 'You are going for an inter-school hockey match.' We stared at him, stunned. 'But sir, we've never played hockey!' was our immediate response. He smiled and said, 'Walk in like you know everything. Take pride in what you do.' And so we did. We stepped onto that field as if we belonged there. And guess what? We won. Whether the other team was trained or not, I will never know. But I do know that belief can sometimes take you further than experience.

Today, when I look at my myriad roles—artist, collector, curator, hostess, mother, movement enthusiast, spiritual seeker—I see echoes of that early permission. I believe Delhi allowed it, school encouraged it, and I thrived in it.

But to live like this, fluidly across several roles, you also need something people rarely talk about: a strong inner structure. While I am largely intuitive, I have also learnt to be intensely disciplined. When I begin a new project, whether curating a show, redesigning a space, or learning something new, I give myself strict timelines. What I am doing, in effect, is building a frame. Not because I want to restrict myself, but because I know my own energy. I know how easily my passion can tip into obsession, how quickly inspiration can consume my nights. A structure helps me flow while staying within it. That way I can build without becoming rigid, and remain open without dissolving.

The Art of Connection

If there is one thing all those early experiences taught me, it is that life doesn't happen in silos. The world isn't neatly divided and neither are we. We are layered, constantly evolving.

Whether in my work or in the people I gather, I have always been guided by the instinct to bring different energies into conversation. If I have been drawn to contrast, it is not for provocation but for the possibility it offers. Whether through collaborations or curatorial moments, I have always believed that true creativity happens at the intersections. Life flows; it overlaps, and sometimes it also collides. If you notice, the most beautiful things often emerge in the spaces in between. Even in my private spaces, be it fundraisers, artist dinners or informal catch-ups, I find joy in bringing people together who might never otherwise meet. A collector, a performer, a writer, a policymaker sitting at the same table. I have witnessed extraordinary conversations between a spiritual teacher and a contemporary dancer, even between a luxury fashion consultant and a grassroots health worker. On paper, they had nothing in common. But when the walls come down, the stories start flowing. What separates them starts to matter less than what they share.

I remember at the MASH Ball, someone said to me, 'I have never seen an event where fashion editors and social workers were actually talking—and not just posing for photographs.' To me, that is the work: to create spaces where genuine, unlikely dialogue can unfold. Where someone from the arts hears about grassroots education, and then asks, 'How can I help?'

That, to me, is what fabulousness should do. While it may shimmer on the outside, it needs to carry something on the inside. I am talking about meaning, about momentum.

Over time, something else has shifted too. People have stopped trying to put me in a box. The art world once questioned why I embraced glamour. The fashion world wondered how I had time for art. But now, I see those same people sharing space, sharing ideas. They have grown more open; just as I have grown more rooted.

That too is the quiet work of a bridge. It may not always be visible, but it is deeply felt. Because when you bring people together, something softens. You see assumptions dissolve, and then you notice what lies beneath surface differences. And beneath it all, people want the same things. They want to live with dignity, they want to feel safe in their skin. They also want to love freely, to build something meaningful, and to imagine a future without limits. It is this everyday hope that drives most lives. There is a common quiet longing to grow, to belong, to flourish. I have found this yearning to be consistent across nationalities, languages, borders, belief systems. People everywhere crave connection, not conflict. It is when these basic human desires are politicized, twisted into tools of power or pulled into identity wars, that something fragile is lost.

That is why I believe it is more important than ever to create spaces of overlap. Not to blur our differences, but to build bridges of understanding across them. That is the quiet, necessary work of a bridge that often begins in the smallest, most personal ways. You need to listen without defensiveness, ask deeper questions, resist the urge to reduce someone to a stereotype based on where they are from or what they wear. It also means refusing to other those who don't mirror your worldview. It means making room for nuance, for divergence, for complexity. It is all about embracing difference and not sameness; about choosing grace over judgement. Essentially, to live and let live, not as a cliché, but as a way of being.

Standing Between Tradition and Modernity

That same instinct to resist binaries has shaped my relationship with tradition and modernity too.

I have noticed how there is often an unspoken, almost tacit understanding that if you are to be seen as modern, you must shed anything that feels too rooted. If you mention rituals, choose not to drink, even speak of God—you are seen as someone who doesn't 'get it'. It is ironic how depth can make you seem outdated.

Friends posing with cigarettes like accessories, holding wine glasses like badges of rebellion, have often said things like, 'Come on, just try it' or 'You don't know what you're missing.' The message was consistent: to belong, you have to blend in.

But I didn't. Not because I wanted to make a point, but because I knew what sat right with me. I wasn't willing to dilute that just to seem cool. People found it hard to believe that I could enjoy myself—fully, freely—without the performance, the props. Sanjay and I never felt deprived. If anything, we would laugh—not at others, but at the absurdity of it all. What is so glamorous about waking up foggy-headed? What is so fabulous about harming your body in the name of fun?

That is not to say it was always easy. Declining with grace takes practice. Sometimes I said no with a smile. At other times, I would try and dodge pressure with humour. Once, I even danced through a party pretending that I was sipping a cocktail and then caught a 4 a.m. flight, glowing. 'What are you on?' a friend asked, surprise written all over her face. My answer? 'Happiness. Sheer joy.'

Maybe this steadfastness came from observing the best. I grew up seeing how you couldn't make my grandmother do anything she didn't want to. People would nudge her to join certain women's gatherings, coax her to chime in with some juicy opinion or weigh in on family gossip. But she would just sit there, poised and unmoved, offering a polite smile, never crossing that line. That kind of integrity left a deep impression on me. It showed me that real elegance is about staying anchored in your truth.

Over the years, I have seen how powerful that can be. While many once discarded traditions in the name of progress, some of those same people have now come full circle. Today, they are doing yoga, consulting *Vastu* experts, speaking of energy and balance as though it were newly discovered. Suddenly, what was once dismissed is desirable.

It makes me smile, not out of smugness, but with quiet relief. Because these things were never passing trends anyway. They are timeless tools that are grounding, always there for those who know how to listen.

That is what I would say to anyone trying to walk that line. You just have to choose your centre. Live from there, and you give others permission to do the same. Being yourself can remind people that it is possible to be spiritual and modern. Stylish and grounded. Generous and boundaried. You don't need to shout it. Just live it and let it be seen.

Being Misunderstood—and Choosing to Bridge Anyway

A gentle caution, though: living at the intersection is often mistaken for indecision, or seen as inconvenient by those who prefer tidy labels. People want to categorize, to fit others into neat boxes in order to simplify what they don't fully grasp. When you don't fit the mould, they start assigning labels. You may be called too bold, too private, too glamorous, too spiritual . . . or simply too much.

I have experienced that. When you are a woman who doesn't perform predictability, who dresses for herself, speaks her mind, you confuse people. And confusion often leads to judgment. But I wasn't trying to confuse anyone. I wasn't trying to prove anything either. I was simply trying to be whole. To honour the many selves within me, be it the artist and the aesthete, the introvert and the leader, or the believer and the disruptor. I didn't see those parts as contradictory. I saw them as facets of the same truth.

Of course, I would have to be living under a rock not to hear the whispers. 'Oh, she's just a socialite,' they say, as if that single word could describe everything that I am. You know what? It makes me smile. Because I am a socialite, perhaps one of the last of a disappearing kind. But not in the way they mean. To me, being a socialite is about bringing people together with purpose. About knowing how to host not just an event, but a moment—one that carries energy, meaning, memory.

Besides, people don't always see the discipline beneath the dazzle. They aren't privy to the years of listening, building, learning and unlearning I have gone through. They haven't seen the quiet choices made away from the spotlight. And that's okay, not everyone needs to understand your life, especially when your life doesn't follow the script they are used to seeing.

Once, during an interview, someone asked me, 'What's that one rumour about yourself you would like to bust?' I smiled and said, 'None. Please believe them all.' There is a certain magic in letting the mystery remain, in letting people wonder. Of course, while they're busy speculating, you can continue doing the work—quietly, consistently, fabulously.

In fact, I've come to believe that being misunderstood is often the price of being original. And if you are truly trying to be a bridge—between disciplines, between generations, between ways of being—then you have to accept that not everyone will be ready to cross with you. But that doesn't mean you stop building. Every time you stay true to yourself, without apology, without dilution, you make it easier for someone else to do the same. And one day, someone who thought they were alone will walk through and realize they are not.

As for me, sometimes, after a long day, I walk through my home and pause in front of a corner that I've rearranged.

It could have a tribal mask beside a neon sculpture, or a minimalist console that is offset by an antique mirror. For me, these aren't just aesthetic choices; these are also conversations that I am curating—between time periods, between energies. In that moment, with a familiar piece whispering something new, I felt truly fabulous. Not because everything is perfect, but because everything is in dialogue.

P.S. A Love Note to Fellow Bridge-Builders

If you have always lived in between cultures, identities, roles, I see you. Perhaps you have never found yourself fitting neatly into a societal box. Maybe you speak many languages, not just literally, but also socially, emotionally, aesthetically. You tend to read a room, to connect the dots.

That is fabulosity. One that is quiet, yet connective and powerful.

Don't ever doubt your value. Don't ever underestimate the quiet strength it takes to stay centred while spanning opposites. Importantly, don't forget to nourish yourself. It is because bridges are not meant to collapse. They are meant to carry life across.

Chapter 9

Connection with the Divine

I speak to the divine the way one might speak to a friend. In the middle of a chaotic day, I often catch myself whispering something. It could be a thought, a fond wish, or a quiet thank you. At times, I even ask, 'Seriously, God? Do I still have to learn this?' The answers always come, not always in words, but in signs, sometimes in dreams, at other times in numbers that repeat. The answers can also come by way of strangers who say things they couldn't possibly know. There is something profoundly intimate about speaking to the divine without formality, without pretence. Over the years, that conversation has only deepened. It has grown quieter, more layered.

If you ask me whether I am religious or spiritual, I'd say I am both. Religion, for me, offers a certain structure that keeps me aligned. There is a science to it, an order that anchors you. But spirituality is the feeling behind the form; the pulse that makes it come alive. If one steadies your steps, the other lights your path. I don't believe you have to choose between the two. Why should you? Religion, simply put, makes it easier to be spiritual. It steadies your inner journey. Spirituality, in turn, transforms religion into something expansive, alive and deeply felt.

Looking back, I realize my spiritual compass was set in childhood, in our home's unique interfaith rhythm. My grandfather followed the teachings of Arya Samaj, while my grandmother was a Sikh. In my mind's eye, I can still hear my grandfather chanting the *Gayatri Mantra* each morning, his voice steady, our heads bowed. Even today, when I repeat that chant, I feel connected not just to him, but also to something much larger than myself.

I also grew up listening to the *Ramayana and the Mahabharata* timeless stories where good triumphed over evil not through might, but through virtue. The message in our home was simple: be a good person, serve the community, pray with sincerity. That was enough.

Only now do I understand how deeply that early atmosphere shaped me. I learnt that the divine wasn't someone to appease, instead someone you could trust completely.

What I also imbibed in those early years was that life isn't random. That every experience, even the painful ones, carries a message. Sometimes it may feel like the universe is offering a gentle slap on the wrist. Other times, it could feel like a quiet hand on the shoulder, guiding you with immense grace.

That foundation, that was soft, inclusive, and heart-led, gave me a language for the divine. Over time, it has grown into a dialogue I carry within me, one that continues to unfold each day.

Sacred Journeys and Energetic Temples

After my marriage, as my spiritual discipline began to take new shape through my husband's deep religiosity, I first stood on the sidelines of his devotion, observing quietly. Slowly, I began to feel its quiet power.

Some people go to temples out of tradition. I go because I need to recharge. Think of it as plugging in a phone running low on battery. These aren't rituals for me; they are recalibrations. Each journey to a sacred place,

I believe, strips away what no longer belongs. It brings me a little closer to my core, a little clearer in spirit.

My visits to Amarnath have been among the most profound. Walking across its uneven terrain, through valleys, over stones, I have felt Lord Shiva in every step. I have felt the landscape itself echoing his presence: the crescent moon in the sky, the stillness in the air, the path like a huge serpent. I remember thinking, *He's walking here too. And I am walking with Him.*

On one such visit, I made a simple request—that the sun not be too hot, too harsh. I just held the thought quietly in my heart. The next thing I knew, the sky shifted. It didn't just drizzle, it poured, a sudden, wild downpour with thunder rolling. For a moment, everyone panicked; we were already halfway along the path. I too was taken aback, until I realized that sometimes, when your prayer is heard deeply enough, even the elements respond.

Another time, at Tirupati, I made the decision to shave my head for the first time. It may not sound like much, but for me it was radical. Up until then, I had always hesitated to trim or cut my hair. I was the girl who wore full sleeves and high necks, who deflected attention from her appearance because she wanted to be seen for her mind, not her skin. But that day, I surrendered. 'Just take care of me,' I whispered, as the first lock of hair fell and, with it, a lone tear. I didn't step out for months after. I ate only *satvik* food. I meditated. I let go. And in that letting go, I felt completely held.

In hindsight, that sense of being held often came to me through temples rooted in masculine energies: Tirupati, Amarnath, Mahakal. These were spaces of discipline, devotion, ascetic stillness. They grounded me, gave structure to my seeking, and brought me a deep sense of spiritual alignment.

But something was shifting quietly beneath the surface. A few years ago, I began feeling drawn to a different kind of energy. It wasn't planned, or even entirely conscious. A series of seemingly random events at this time nudged me towards Shakti temples—Jwalamukhi, Kamakhya, Kalighat. At the time, I didn't question it. I simply followed the pull.

It was only later, with reflection, that I understood. I had been living in a state of constant doing. There is often an unspoken pressure to toughen up, to take on more masculine traits in order to be taken seriously. What was missing in me, I now see, was softness and receptivity: the holding energy of the feminine. The divine always knows what you need long before you do. And in its quiet wisdom, it was guiding me back into balance.

At the temple of Kalighat, I found myself crying, not from sadness, but from something deeper. The energy was so pure, so potent, it moved through me like a wave, flushing out what I hadn't even known I was carrying.

That's the thing about sacred places. You don't choose them, they choose you. They summon you when you are ready either to release or to receive. Even when I travel for work, I find myself veering towards a temple, a shrine, a sacred corner tucked somewhere. It is as if the soul already knows where to go long before the body follows.

I have stood in front of the Shroud of Turin in Italy, tears streaming down my face. Just as I have felt rooted before Shiva temples, the energy so magnetic I couldn't move. It was as if my body knew it had to stay still and listen. Once, while I was in a sanctum, my phone overheated from the charge in the air. Such places carry a frequency, a vibration. Yes, you can pray anywhere, and I do. But there are certain places where prayer feels amplified, where the universe is leaning in just a little bit more.

People often ask me why I return to temples so often. The answer is simple: they strip away everything that isn't essential. They remind me of who I am beneath the layers. To me, that is the most fabulous version of myself. The one who bows to divine power and feels completely free.

Faith and the Power of Miracles

People often speak of faith as if it were an abstract concept, something you either possess or lack. But for me, faith is visceral. I have felt it in my bones, in my breath, in the stillness that follows surrender. Especially in those moments when logic failed, and the only thing left was prayer.

I remember a time when my thyroid levels were rising. A specialist had been tracking them for months, and his verdict was clear: I needed to start medication urgently. I resisted, perhaps because my mother had struggled with thyroid medicine. It was a defiance of sorts, a belief that I would cure it with alternate means.

So I did what felt most natural. I went to Tirupati. I sat in the temple, breathing deeply, silently asking for healing. I wasn't bargaining or pleading. I was simply surrendering.

A few days later, I repeated my tests and sent them to the doctor. He called, stunned. 'Have you visited another doctor and changed your medication while you have been consulting me for months? he asked. 'Your results are normal,' he said incredulously. Of course, I hadn't changed the medication. In fact, nothing had changed except that one hour I had spent in prayer.

'Then this is a miracle,' he said. And I knew he was right.

Another time, during the pandemic, I prayed for something far more specific. I had gone to the Mahakal temple, one of the twelve Jyotirlingas. I sat quietly near the *kund* and prayed not for success or health, but for the elimination of ego. I had been doing charity work, trying to live with an open heart. But I could still feel traces of ego within me. I wanted to be free of it. So I asked the divine sincerely, vulnerably: 'Please take this away. Burn the last of it. I don't want to live with this anymore.'

That night, my body began to swell. By 4 a.m., the entire left side of my body, my feet, hands, face had puffed up severely. At first, I thought it was some kind of an allergic reaction. I consulted doctors across cities, and underwent every possible test. Over a period of time, I eliminated gluten, dairy from my diet. Even switched detergents. Nothing seemed to work. The blood reports were clean. The swelling, however, would come and go—five days of inflammation, two days of rest. Over and over again, the pattern would repeat on different parts of the body

There were days I could not walk. And yet, I continued working. I was shooting for magazines and for some of my designer friends during this time, often filming only from one side of my face.

Eventually, I consulted a few spiritual teachers. One of them looked at me and said, 'Mahakal is a powerful force of manifestation. When you ask from the heart, the universe listens. Not always gently.'

And suddenly, with his words, everything made sense. My body was not betraying me. It was following the instructions my soul had whispered. After almost a year, just as suddenly as it had begun, the swelling disappeared. The reports, all the while, stayed normal. There was no diagnosis. What can I say except that it was grace.

That experience taught me two things. One, that intentions carry immense power. And the second, that transformation isn't always elegant. It can be uncomfortable, inconvenient, but it is always sacred.

These weren't isolated events either. There have been so many moments where signs have appeared as gentle confirmations. Once, I had to walk unexpectedly far to reach a temple. While on the way, I found myself questioning the purpose of the detour. As I was walking, I looked up and saw a large poster with the words *television winner and Oscar* written on it. I don't know why, but it felt like a message, a wink from the universe. Some might call it a coincidence. I call it a connection.

One of the most profound moments came during the pandemic, when my mother was hospitalized in a critical state. The doctors called my sister and me into a room and showed us her intestines. I remember feeling frozen. I've never been good with medical matters. I didn't know what questions to ask or what steps to take. I told my sister I would do what I knew: I went to the temple to pray.

As I sat on the temple stairs after my prayers, trying to steady my breath, out of nowhere, I noticed a man walking up to me, someone I didn't know. He introduced himself as the contractor of the work that was in progress at the temple. In the course of the conversation, he even asked that some help be rendered towards replacing the metal pipes of the temple. I agreed without thinking. Later that day, I realized how strange that encounter had been. My mother was battling a severe intestinal issue and here was a stranger speaking of pipes, asking for help. Something about it felt orchestrated, as though the divine was speaking in signs.

That night, things began to shift. It may sound unbelievable, but that's how miracles often work. If your faith is steady, the signs come. And when they do, they are impossible to ignore. I have learned not to question them at all. When I believe, things align. When I doubt, I tend to stagnate.

Most of all, I have come to realize that faith isn't always about getting what you want. It's about receiving what your soul needs.

Karma, Forgiveness, and Grace

I often say I don't hold grudges, light-heartedly adding that they are bad for the skin. Of course they are, no question about it. But beneath that statement lies something far more serious: a deep belief in karma, one I have spoken of before.

I don't think any of us escapes our actions. What you put out into the world, your thoughts, your words, your intentions, everything comes back. I have seen it too often, in too many subtle and startling ways, to dismiss it as a coincidence. Karma isn't just some abstract law to me; it's a living force.

That is why I try not to retaliate when I am hurt. Not because I am some saint, but because I don't want to stay stuck in the karmic cycle. When someone wrongs you and you hit back with words, with anger, with revenge, you are only strengthening the bond between you. You are falling into the karmic spiral. But if you break the cycle, if you let it go and walk away, you have freed yourself. You have moved on. That, to me, is real power. Remember how my friends call me a Karma Collector?

There was a time in my life when I witnessed, almost too clearly, the karmic consequences that followed those who had wronged me. It wasn't because I wished it upon them, but because that is how karma works. What you put out eventually finds its way back. Seeing that unfold was sobering. It made me deeply aware of my own thoughts, especially in moments of hurt or anger. That is why today I try not to speak ill of anyone. I block the memory, I move on, I forget. I refuse to let someone else's darkness take up space in my life or shape the karma I create.

Forgiveness, for me, therefore, isn't about being noble. It's about protecting my energy, my time, my peace. I often say I practise selective amnesia, not as a performance, but as a discipline. I truly forget what does not serve me. If someone hurt me years ago, chances are I have erased the details. My friends may bring up incidents and I will blink, completely blank. Not because I am pretending, but because I have chosen not to carry that weight.

After the Netflix series aired, messages trickled in from people I knew. They said things like, 'Now we understand why you stayed silent' or 'Your restraint made sense to us in a new way.' I had not expected that. But it reaffirmed something I have always believed, that when you move with grace, you don't need to explain yourself. In time, the truth reveals itself. Sometimes grace is indeed the most fabulous response of all.

When people ask how I stay peaceful, how I remain centred despite noise, gossip and conflict, my answer is simple. I trust that the universe is watching, and that no cruelty, no injustice, no betrayal goes unseen.

On a lighter note, having 100 clips on your head helps in keeping you balanced too!

Protecting the Sacred in a Noisy World

Spirituality, for me, has always been deeply personal and never meant for display. In today's world, where everything gets captioned and uploaded, I find myself resisting the urge to share the sacred. Not because I am secretive, but because I believe certain things lose their power when spoken in the wrong setting.

There have been times at parties when someone, holding a drink in one hand, leaned over and said, 'Tell me about your spiritual practices. I want to start something too.' I usually smile and reply, 'This isn't the place.' If someone is genuinely interested, they can message me later and I'll be sure to help however I can. But not while loud music is playing, or people are gossiping at the next table. You can't talk about spirituality between bites of sushi and selfies. It feels wrong. My time, my energy, and especially my spiritual frequency, are sacred to me. I have worked hard to keep them clean.

Over the years, people have come to sense that about me. Even in loud cities and busy circles, there is an invisible boundary around me. I don't announce it; it's just there. People know not to bring me petty talk or mean-spirited jokes. Not because I am judgemental, but because I won't participate. It is not who I am.

Some might think that's isolating. But for me, it's freedom. When you stop engaging with the noise, you start hearing your own rhythm more clearly. You are not performing, you are present.

I have never wanted a spiritual life that is performative. I want one that is real, rooted and also quietly radiant.

Living as a Vessel of the Divine

When I think about true radiance, I think of serenity that asks for nothing and yet fills the room. When I sit in meditation, I often see Buddha's face with his blissful expression. His eyes are neither open nor closed. The face isn't smiling, but it isn't neutral either. It is suspended in stillness, pure, whole, at peace.

I have seen that same peace in the paintings of goddesses, in the meditative postures of Shiva, in the slow, circular gestures of temple dancers. There is a kind of self-absorption there that is not rooted in ego, but in essence. The quiet absorption of someone anchored in themselves. Not reaching outward, but glowing from within. I have come to believe that glow can only come from spiritual discipline.

There was a time when I divided myself. There was the spiritual part, the aesthetic part, the public part. But now, there are no such divisions. My life is one continuous thread. I don't practise spirituality and then move on. It lives in everything—what I eat, where I go, what I wear, how I speak, who I spend time with, what I give my energy to. Whether I am stepping into a temple or onto a red carpet, I try to carry the same intention.

That is what I mean when I say I want to be a vessel. I believe we are all given certain tools—a voice, a body, influence, intuition. And if we don't use them consciously, they start using us.

There is also a responsibility that comes with living this way. You stop performing and start listening. Not to what the world expects, but to what the divine might hear.

That is the life I try to lead now. A life not divided, but integrated. A life where every gesture is an offering, every act a form of *seva*. Where the sacred isn't a place I visit, but something I carry within me. Because to me, that is what real fabulosity is.

Chapter 10

Fabulously Ever After

It is almost a given that at some point you will be asked what kind of legacy you want to leave behind. It is the kind of question people love to ask near the end of an interview, or ponder in the final pages of a book. I understand why. It offers a sense of closure. A legacy sounds grand, final, noble.

I have, however, never seen legacy as one big defining act. To me, legacy lives in the small, quieter things as much as in the grand gestures. It lives in the choices you make when no one is watching or applauding. It reflects in how you speak to someone who has nothing to offer you. It is seen in how you hold space for another's truth without rushing to fix it. It is about showing up on time, even when no one is keeping score. Over time, it is these seemingly small things that leave a mark. That, to me, comprises real legacy.

When I think of the people who shaped me—my grandmother, my parents, my teachers, the quiet mentors—I remember how they made me feel seen, safe and inspired. I realize that feeling need not be reserved for deep or lifelong relationships alone. For instance, I was pleasantly surprised to experience it in the most unexpected place: on the sets of *Bigg Boss*.

I remember that set distinctly. There was a hum of anticipation in the air, that unmistakable charge that television productions carry. And then, like the scene had been waiting for its cue, Salman Khan entered, carrying with him an effortless charisma. At that moment, it seemed like the energy in the room had lifted. Before I realized it, he began introducing me with such grace that the noise around me seemed to fade. The warmth with which he spoke about my journey—my three weeks in the public eye as opposed to his three decades—was humbling, to say the least. In that one moment, I didn't merely feel like a guest on a show. And truly, that is what legacy is about. It is not how long you have shone, but how graciously you make space for someone else's spark.

The funny thing about legacy is that you never quite know where it will land or who it will quietly reach. You just live with intention and let the impact shape itself. I have had people walk up to me and say, 'That one thing you said to me years ago . . . it stayed with me. I didn't fully understand it then, but it shifted something.' I have had mothers write to me and say, 'I stepped away to raise my children. I never thought I would feel visible again. But after seeing you, I feel a spark of hope. I have signed up for a class. I am brushing up on an old skill. I am remembering a version of myself I thought I'd lost.'

Feedback like this leaves me speechless. It is a reminder that legacy doesn't only live in boardrooms or headlines. It lives just as powerfully in kitchens and classrooms, in bedtime stories and in sacrifices no one applauds. When a woman finds the courage to reclaim her visibility, not just in the world's eyes, but in her own, that is a legacy too. Over time, I have come to realize that legacy often reveals itself in the most unassuming ways. That is why I never underestimate the ripple effect of the smallest gesture, even the ones you don't remember making.

But while I treasure these moments, I don't let praise settle too deep in my bones. I receive it with gratitude, and then I let it go. Not because I am modest, but because if I stop to bask in glory, I am sure to lose momentum. So instead, I move forward to the next project. About creating again, becoming again. I believe that the goal is never just to finish with a flourish or gloating over one milestone, however grand it may be. I have therefore always been more interested in what's still forming; what is yet to come.

Even in Cannes, a place where everything around me screamed glamour and applause, I didn't pause. Sure, it was a flex to be there, dressed in couture, walking the red carpet, with the camera chasing every single move and the world watching. But I was sure that I hadn't gone there to bask in the spotlight. I had gone as a learner, and most importantly, as someone carrying a message from my country.

In the midst of all this, it took someone to remind me to slow down. 'You're in Cannes,' the voice said. 'Relax. Take a breath. This is the moment of a lifetime. Go ahead and enjoy it.' To be honest, I did take the advice and pause. For five minutes, I allowed myself to soak it in. I looked around, savoured my surroundings and told myself, 'This is beautiful. It feels so good to be here.' And then, I picked up my bag and continued to walk, my thoughts already veering towards my next project. Fabulousness, for me, is about the rush of possibilities, the excitement of starting again. That is what keeps me creatively alive.

Don't get me wrong. This mindset isn't about being restless. It's only about staying curious and connected to that spark and seeing it turn into fire.

What also keeps me moving is the refusal to be defined by any single role. I am an artist, a collector, a philanthropist, a mother, an aspiring singer, an aspiring actor. Yes, I am all of that and also none of it. Because I believe in leaving space for reinvention. Not as a dramatic overhaul, but as a daily practice. I need to be comfortable with unfamiliarity, to be able to say, 'Okay, who am I becoming now?'

There was a time when I carried a quiet regret of not having attended formal art school. In fact, I would often find myself wondering if that gap made me any less of an artist. That ache returned like an unrequited dream, the way unrequited love lingers long after it is gone. Over the years, however, I have come to appreciate how my life became its own kind of curriculum. Had I walked the traditional art school road, I might never have been able to carve out the path that I have. The one that has led me to where I am today, to my collection, my photography, my foundation.

To anyone who holds a similar regret, I want them to know that your legacy isn't built from the road you missed, but from how fiercely you walked the road you chose.

Cities, Symbols, and What Endures

Speaking of the paths we take, I am reminded that sometimes you are shaped not just by people or experiences, but also by places. Cities, especially, have left their imprint on me. They have changed the way I see beauty, resilience, even faith. Each city you visit leaves its own residue within you, something you tend to carry with you long after you have moved on.

In the early '90s, I remember walking through Rome with a sense of wonder. It was as if everything that I had so far studied in history and art books had come alive before me, in all its splendour. I think what Rome taught me was that history isn't just the past, it's really about the presence.

Walking through the city, I also learnt another important lesson—that beauty doesn't fade just because time passes.

In Paris, the lesson was different. The French, of course, have a way of doing things with style and quiet confidence. From art shows to fashion weeks, there is a level of curation and aesthetic discipline unmatched anywhere. The city reminded me that tradition and innovation don't have to clash, that they can coexist and flow together.

Mumbai has always been my eternal spark. It is alive with energy, ambition and unapologetic drive. It is a promised land, a city of dreams. If you are relentless enough, you can build something lasting here. There is a pulse to Mumbai that never stills, a rhythm that urges you to keep moving, keep becoming. To grow in a place like this without losing your roots, that, to me, is also the quiet art of legacy.

And then there's the city of Banaras. I wouldn't even call it a city. I have said before how it feels more like a divine stage, a cosmic Broadway theatre. You don't walk through Banaras; you simply surrender to its fascinating sights and sounds. I am particularly drawn to its symphony of sound and silence. I love the clang of temple bells as much as the hush of dawn on the ghats. And then there are the chants that echo like a heartbeat. It is enchanting to witness how the city keeps shifting from sunrise to twilight yet its soul remains unchanged. To me, the biggest lesson that the city offers is that life and death are not opposites, but part of a greater harmony.

I remember being in Venice once, and something about that city reminded me of Banaras. Perhaps it was the water, or the rituals woven into everyday life. When I mentioned it to Anish Kapoor, the celebrated sculptor, the connection felt affirmed.

In Ladakh, it was humbling to witness the unforgiving climate. Yet, despite it, life simply continues to move with grace. It truly made me sit up and reflect on the intrinsic quality of endurance, of resilience in human beings. True resilience often doesn't announce itself, does it? It simply gets on with the work at hand.

Bhutan gave me a different, equally enduring lesson. I remember being inside a monastery when a group of women came up to me and gently touched my skirt.

I assumed they were asking me for money. Just then, the guide leaned in towards me and whispered something that left me in awe. 'They are blessing you,' he said. That one simple sentence shifted something in me. It made me realize how grace can arrive in several forms and shapes, and through gestures that ask for nothing in return.

I had another awe-inspiring experience in Bhutan. I was staying at a luxury hotel when I noticed stray dogs lounging within the property. At one point, I saw them sprawled peacefully near the pool. No one shooed them away. The hotel staff simply said, 'If they come, we let them.' It was a quiet act of coexistence that moved me beyond measure. In that moment, I was reminded that legacy isn't just about what you build, it is about the space you make for other beings.

And finally, there is Delhi, my home. It is the city I am rooted in. Delhi, for me, is where memory and momentum meet. It is the place where the girl I once was and the woman I became coexist. A city layered with culture, it is also where my creative impulses have found form—on walls and canvases, in collections and conversations. I would go so far as to say Delhi grounds me. It reminds me that while fabulousness can be fluid and far-reaching, it must have an anchor. For me, that anchor will always be here.

These cities I have walked, these energies I have carried home, they have shaped me in ways no camera or canvas can fully capture. But maybe, just maybe, through storytelling, visual, emotional, spiritual, I can one day pass that on.

When the Heart Says Yes

While all these places left something behind in me, they also opened something up. They offered me new ways of seeing, of trusting, of moving through the world with a little more openness. Over time, I have come to realize that legacy isn't just built through what you hold onto, it is shaped by what you let in. And most of the time, that means listening to your instinct, even when it defies logic. Especially when it does.

Let me tell you a story. We were staying at the Martinez Hotel in Cannes, where access is tightly guarded during the festival. On my first day there, I heard a knock on our suite door. Standing outside was a young blonde model, stunning and clearly distressed. She explained that her friend wasn't answering the door at her hotel, that she had to get ready for the red carpet, and asked if she could change in our room.

I didn't have the heart to say no. She looked sincere. We let her in, gave her some space, and she quietly changed and left. An hour later, I stepped outside to see her taking pictures on the hotel steps. Soon, it became clear that many people were trying to find ways to sneak into the hotel just to get those coveted photos on the iconic Martinez steps. Some even tried bribing my hair and makeup team to get in.

Later, my team warned me: 'Ma'am, please don't do that again. You can't be so trusting. Random people will try to get in.' While I nodded in agreement—what they were saying was logical—here's the thing: if that incident were to repeat, I would still end up doing it again. Because at that moment, I was reminded of something important, of how privileged I am to be able to access spaces like these. For her, that moment was a break. For me, it was a mirror.

If anything, it affirmed something I have always believed, that legacy is not about the doors you walk through, but the ones you hold open for someone else.

That said, being generous doesn't mean being blind. Over the years, I have learnt the need to draw clear boundaries, even while staying open-hearted. In the past, there were occasions when I held on to friendships that were rooted in obligation, not mutual growth. At the time, I thought walking away would make me cruel. But increasingly I realize that this kind of kindness can deplete you beyond measure. Sometimes the most compassionate thing you can do is to take a giant step back. You need to be at peace with your own values and make choices from that place.

There is one lesson I return to often. It is not to let discomfort drown out the message. If you are experiencing emotional unease or even physical pain, there is usually something underneath, waiting to be heard. In these moments, I pause and ask myself, *What is this here to teach me?* Sometimes the answer is courage. Sometimes it is a restraint. But always, it is growth. Some life lessons even stretch across years, reappearing in new ways. You may find yourself wondering, 'Why is this happening again and again? Why are patterns repeating? What am I not seeing?' The universe, I believe, is very patient. It will keep sending you the same lesson, dressed in different forms, until you finally learn from it. The only way to graduate to the next chapter in life is not to resist discomfort, but to work your way through it. That is when the story truly shifts.

If there is one group I hold close when I think about these shifts, it is young women in all phases of their lives. The ones finding their voice in boardrooms, or the ones simply trying to stay soft in a hard world. The loud ones, the tired ones, the ones still figuring it all out.

If you are reading this, I want to say that you don't need to shrink to be accepted. You don't need to make yourself smaller to make others comfortable. Through all this, guard your emotional energy like it is sacred, and do not forget to honour your intuition even when it is inconvenient. Above all, don't wait for permission to shine. And if at times it feels like you don't have a blueprint for the path you want to tread, that is okay. After all, there are no rules of architecture for building castles in the clouds. Dream anyway.

What I Hope Lingers

As for my dreams, there are many, several still unfolding. The one thing people often ask me is, 'Will we see you on screen again?' Well, definitely, if the right opportunity comes along. The camera is a powerful thing. I would even go as far as to say that it can be addictive. There is an intimacy about it that draws you in. When I am in front of it, I forget the millions watching. Instead, I only see that one lens. It is amazing how, if you can tune out the noise and the pressure, it becomes a space of pure presence. And sometimes, just showing up as yourself, unfiltered, unapologetic, is the boldest thing you can do.

One such moment came when Aryan Khan invited me to do a cameo in his debut directorial series. I was in Doha when his name flashed on my phone. Hearing him say that he wanted me to be part of his vision was quietly overwhelming. It had to be, since I have watched him grow from a young boy into a creative force. To now witness his craft up close was like coming full circle; it was both moving and awe-inspiring. He is an exceptionally talented young man—calm, focused, involved in every single detail on set, right from costumes to lighting. Being on his set, I felt like a star in an entirely new way. Not because of the spotlight, but because of the care, the trust. That kind of creative invitation is rare, and I will always hold it close.

It also made me reflect on the kind of stories I now want to help tell. Stories of resilience in the storm, beauty in decay, generosity without agenda. Stories that inspire, uplift, remind us who we were before the world told us who to be. Because history is usually written by those who win—and too often, that perspective erases every other. Indian art and culture, for instance, were more often than not framed through a colonial lens. I want to tell stories about India in all its layered, vibrant glory.

I also dream of building something lasting, a museum, perhaps. A space that honours Indian art and craft. A space where the tactile, the handmade, and the deeply storied are treated with the reverence they deserve. It will be a place where past and future speak to each other. A place where heritage isn't boxed away, but brought to life. I believe our culture and traditions root us. And without that anchor, a society drifts.

I want to make films about women too. About our strength, our softness, our complexities. Stories that shift something. Stories that hold up a mirror to the soul. I often hear my inner voice whispering, 'The time has come'—that curious phrase from Lewis Carroll's *The Walrus and the Carpenter*, where they discuss how it's time 'to talk of many things'. For me, these things are the stories that matter most: stories of Indian culture and heritage, stories of women. In short, stories that stir the soul awake.

And maybe, long after I am gone, someone will come across a photograph, a film, a handcrafted object I helped preserve, and feel something stir within them. Not because it was mine, but because it made them remember their own light.

That, to me, would be the most fabulous ending of all—a lasting legacy.

Acknowledgements

This book is a celebration of all those who have shaped me and stood by me through every season of life.

My grandmother who taught me the quiet strength of stillness. She stood her ground like a mountain, graceful yet unshakeable, untouched by material desires. She remains the closest I have known to a saint in spirit. My grandfather who embodied duty and integrity. A pillar of his community, he led with wisdom, generosity and fairness, often the calm voice resolving others' storms.

From my father, I have inherited an endless curiosity and creative drive. He has taught me that passion and perseverance can build anything. My mother showed me the power of compassion. Her boundless care for family and friends shaped my understanding of love. Even when I resisted her ways, I came to realize how much of her lives within me. My brother and sister have surrounded me with unwavering faith and love, their belief in me constant and unconditional.

In Sanjay, I found my anchor, mirror and constant companion—a parent, husband and friend rolled into one. His quiet strength has steadied me through every high and low. And Robin, who with his warmth, honesty and affectionate humour, lights up my days. I love how he advises me about the world, telling me I'm not worldly enough, even though neither of us truly are.

My parents-in-law have been a blessing. My mother-in-law's grace and generosity opened my world to new experiences, while my father-in-law's quiet perfectionism reminded me of my own father. I cherished our conversations and the wisdom I found in his company.

Last but not the least, the city of Mumbai will forever be my eternal muse. A city whose pulse keeps me awake and inspired. It has given me both grit and grace, and the courage to begin again.

My heartfelt thanks to Preeti Chaturvedi of The Sunflower Seeds, who first sowed the idea for this book and nurtured it with care and conviction. And to the wonderful team at Penguin Random House India, particularly Milee Ashwarya and Rinku Paul, for their unstinting support and partnership in bringing this vision to life. Thanks also to Yash Daiv and Aakriti Khurana for their relentless efforts across multiple drafts and cover versions.